What people are saying about

Event Horizon

In *Event Horizon*, Rambatan and Johanssen combine Lacanian psychoanalysis and various critical theory approaches for the analysis of how the mindset of the Alt-Right has shaped the contemporary internet. The resulting st 'y is an excellent must-read for everyone who wants to   nd how the subject thinks and acts in contempora   lism.
Professor Christian Fuch   *edia: A Critical Introduction* and *Digi*   *an Capitalism in the Age of Trump* r

Event Horizon calls   the contemporary internet and networked AI in   of a new erotic. Working within the Lacanian tradition, the book pairs interpretation of classic sources with critical foresight on all matters digital. This theory manifesto provides an alternative framework that relates memes, selfies and online dating to rising heteropessimism and fascism. What should be the response when cuteness flips into violence? The authors' cautious motto: we are all part of the problem, but there are solutions. I'd say: vulnerable universality, bring it on!
Professor Geert Lovink, Institute of Network Cultures, author of *Sad by Design: On Platform Nihilism*

Event Horizon is a unique and most compellingly written book, composed – not unlike a piece of music – of a radical dystopia and an equally radical utopia. The first part presents us with powerful and pitiless analysis of the predicaments of our present social order, focusing particularly on how digital technology informs and shapes our lives and our social bonds in all their multiple aspects. But then, in the last part, it does not

simply turn against technology, but envisions its involvement in a very different kind of social tie. Sexuality and its 'beyond', or transformation, are put at the center of this transformative revolution, which we are invited to imagine as the only Real on our horizon, with 'love or death' as our only choice.
Professor Alenka Zupančič, author of *What Is Sex?*

This bristling little book embarks on nothing less than a total diagnosis of our sick capitalist present. Rambatan and Johanssen cut right to the chase in their incisive reading of forms of contemporary enjoyment online, disclosing a mutation in Lacan's four discourses.
Professor Sianne Ngai, author of *Theory of the Gimmick: Aesthetic Judgment and Capitalist Form*

Also by the authors

Johanssen, Jacob (2019). *Psychoanalysis and Digital Culture: Audiences, Social Media, and Big Data*. Routledge.
UK: 9781138484443

Rambatan, Bonni, and Johanssen, Jacob (2013). *Cyborg Subjects: Discourses on Digital Culture*. CreateSpace Publishing.
UK: 9781491271513

For further discussion and supplementary materials about the book's themes, please visit: http://bit.ly/readEH

Event Horizon

Sexuality, Politics, Online Culture, and the Limits of Capitalism

Event Horizon

Sexuality, Politics, Online Culture,
and the Limits of Capitalism

Bonni Rambatan
& Jacob Johanssen

Winchester, UK
Washington, USA

JOHN HUNT PUBLISHING

First published by Zero Books, 2021
Zero Books is an imprint of John Hunt Publishing Ltd., No. 3 East St., Alresford,
Hampshire SO24 9EE, UK
office@jhpbooks.com
www.johnhuntpublishing.com
www.zero-books.net

For distributor details and how to order please visit the 'Ordering' section on our website.

Text copyright: Bonni Rambatan and Jacob Johanssen 2020

ISBN: 978 1 78904 876 6
978 1 78904 877 3 (ebook)
Library of Congress Control Number: 2021930333

A CIP catalogue record for this book is available from the British Library.

Design: Stuart Davies

UK: Printed and bound by CPI Group (UK) Ltd, Croydon, CR0 4YY
Printed in North America by CPI GPS partners

We operate a distinctive and ethical publishing philosophy in
all areas of our business, from our global network of authors to
production and worldwide distribution.

Contents

Introduction

Into the Digital Black Hole

The Event Horizon Metaphor

In astrophysics, an Event Horizon refers to the outermost periphery of a black hole, located a Schwarzchild radius away from its centre. It is a point of no return, beyond which nothing, not even light, can escape. Crossing the Event Horizon from the outside brings us into a strange reality, where time and space switch places. Inside the black hole, space behaves like time, in that it can only move forward in one direction at a certain speed: Just as time can only move from the past to the future, the time-like space beyond the Event Horizon can only move to the direction of the spacetime singularity. Once we enter, we will inevitably be integrated into the singularity in a spectacular, spaghettified death—that is, if we somehow manage to survive the crushing force of gravity before it. Obversely, time behaves like space: inside the black hole, we can see light coming from both the past and the future, i.e. light coming into and light trying (and failing) to escape from the black hole.

For many of us, this is what capitalism feels like. We are moving forward, unable to resist, almost as if by violent force of nature, towards the direction of technological singularity. There can only be two options: We will either achieve singularity, our minds uploaded into tragic immortality as we completely lose our subjectivity, or get crushed by the immense chaos of economic, social, and environmental collapse before we even manage to get anywhere near there.

The phrase also has a secondary meaning. The philosophical Event, most notably developed by Alain Badiou (2006), refers to an ontological rupture from which a new structure of Being is possible. Through its rupture, the Event also opens up a new

1

universe. The Event is a revolution which overturns all existing order and structures. It gives birth to a new sense of reality. That which was before invisible or excluded has come to the surface. The horizon of such an Event thus means the moment where we begin to see the first glimmers of light on these elements.

Event Horizon is also the name of a 1997 science-fiction horror film, directed by Paul W. S. Anderson. Set in 2047, the film follows a crew who embark on a rescue mission of the titular lost spaceship, Event Horizon. Upon its discovery, the crew learn that the spaceship was used for secret experiments with a newly developed engine which generates a wormhole used to link up two points in spacetime in order to speed up space travel. It would fold spacetime so that the point from where the spaceship originates and the point to where it should travel overlap. This gateway lies behind three rotating magnetic rings which align to create the wormhole. However, the experiments failed and the gateway, by its own doing, formed a rift in the spacetime continuum. The spaceship went beyond the universe and was found, 7 years after its disappearance, orbiting Neptune.

As they explore the Event Horizon, the crew discover that the ship has acquired an ability to feel and exhibit a level of consciousness. 'The ship brought back something with it, a life force of some kind!' remarks Starck, one officer. 'It knows my fears, it knows my secrets,' says Miller, the commanding officer. Like many horror movies that depict a mysterious power, it tells of a force that desires to pull the ship back into the Lacanian Real—the traumatic realm beyond consciousness and language—and to possess its crew members. In a sense, the desire to subject the laws of physics into the ultimate utilitarian tool of humanity arrives in its true form: as the desire for the Law to recognise the needs and desires of the Subject.[1] Can we not draw an analogy to contemporary technology such as ubiquitous surveillance, Big Data, and Artificial Intelligence here? As we go on to discuss in the coming chapters, we live in an age where technology itself is said to be able to access the Real and surpass its own capabilities in doing so. Our networked, code-based, algorithm-driven, smart-functioning devices, apps, platforms, and ways of communicating and behaving are allegedly always improving and will continue to get closer to recognising our true desires.

The crew go on to discover that the original crew on the Event Horizon engaged in a kind of possessed, naked sado-masochistic orgy which led to them killing each other. As they go aboard the Event Horizon, the rescue crew too are possessed by the ship's force of sentience. They begin to hallucinate individuals and past experiences from their lives. Their own repressed traumas return and seem to be forced upon them by the supernatural character of the spaceship. While our current state of technology and politics has not yet degraded into a full-blown sex murder party, it is not difficult to see that violence, harassment, perversion, trauma, hate, and extremism characterise much of our online life today as meanings become increasingly obsolete. The ship, the representation of our contemporary technology, comes to embody a Law that has the power to reinforce but also to redeem our repressed guilt and anxieties. The film, then, is an astute portrayal of subjectivity in the Lacanian sense: in our search for the 'seductive gravity' of enjoyment (Chabin 2018, 88), we are always threatened by and drawn to the traumatic force of the Other's desire that pulls us towards the Real.

A Very Brief Introduction to Lacanian Psychoanalysis[2]

But why Lacan? In his emphasis on language and its relation to the unconscious, we argue that Lacan provides the best framework to analyse a culture so heavily reliant on code and imagery. For Lacan, the unconscious is famously structured like a language—both are held together in a twisted relationship of presences and absences, zeroes and ones. The unconscious is formed as a kind of side effect upon the Subject's entry into the Symbolic Order, Lacan's term for the structure of language, norms, values, and social relations which acts upon the Subject. Any attempt at language, i.e. speaking or writing, for the Subject is centred on something that is excluded which the Subject nonetheless tries to articulate. 'This unsaid—i.e. that which eludes symbolisation and only comes about through symbolisation—is the unconscious—an unconscious that, enigmatically, is outside and, at the same time, inside language' (Krüger & Johanssen 2016, 21).

While the unconscious is the effect of the Symbolic Order (and how something in the unconscious is rendered conscious), language is also one of the existential conditions of the unconscious in its structural sense; it is foundational for the unconscious. 'The unconscious is a process of signification that is beyond our control; it is the language that speaks through us rather than the language we speak' (Homer 2005, 44). The unconscious is the discourse of the Other, to quote a well-known Lacanian aphorism. Language forms the intimate core of the Subject that nonetheless comes from a place external to it. There is always a lack that remains in the Other, and the Subject is that which occupies this lack.

This notion is key for Lacan, as he developed it in numerous ways. A core development takes place in relation to sexuality. As we outline in Chapter 4, the sexual non-relation denotes the interconnections between the Symbolic and sexuality. As the famous Lacanian saying goes: 'There is no sexual relationship' (Lacan 1999, 193). By this statement, he meant that there is no originary sexual relation between subjects which would be characterised by notions we commonly associate with sexuality: union, complementarity, or transcendence. Instead, sexuality is an ontology that is based on primal repression. There is no pure or foundational form of sexuality, because it is always already part of the Symbolic, of particular signifying chains. Sexuality is always the sexuality of the Other, both actual and imagined.

It is often messy, contradictory, and problematic, but also pleasurable and arousing because subjects can cover over the non-relation through certain practices, speech acts, ideologies, and other signifiers that inform particular sexual fantasies. Sexuality is inherently contradictory and lacking as it brings forward the inseparability of the Symbolic Order and *jouissance* in their very heterogeneity (Zupančič 2017).

The fundamental lack at the heart of the Subject is both sustained and forever tried to be filled through desire. Desire too originates in the Other; the Subject is driven by the desire to desire. Desire can never be satisfied and seeks to find the unobtainable object (*objet a*, the object-cause of desire) which the subject was deprived of upon their entering into the Symbolic realm. This object comes into being as a result of the lack in the Other. The baby eventually realises that the Other (e.g. the mother) is lacking and cannot completely fulfil their desires. Throughout their life, the Subject feels that something is missing or not quite right and, often unconsciously, seeks to fill this void through particular fantasies and actions (consuming commodities, posting on social media, engaging in romance, etc.). Affects borne of this never-ending desire are called *jouissance*, or surplus-enjoyment; desire marks a surplus of enjoyment which is never pure or fully enjoyable, but rather takes the form of pleasure-pain. While *jouissance* often involves pleasurable sensations, they often involve feelings of shame, guilt, thrill, hurt, heartbreak, discomfort, and other emotions, as they all pertain to the sustenance of desire. All of these work hand-in-hand with the capitalist injunction to consume, which the superego relays to the Subject. Enjoyment in capitalism can take many forms, and we outline various kinds in relation to technology in this book.

The notion of the Symbolic was also fruitfully developed by Lacan in relation to his discourses. The term 'discourse' denotes a social bond which is established via language and other

Symbolic relations. As we outline in Chapter 1, there are four principle discourses which designate different types of social relations, plus a mutated one under capitalism. A discourse, in its socio-political specificity, shapes the Subject's inter- and intra-subjective relations between themself and the wider structures of society, the kind of reality they experience. A discourse determines knowledge production and shapes particular forms of speech. As such, a discourse is an empty structuring device that makes the frame for particular epistemologies and ideologies through which they are expressed.

Apart from the Symbolic, the Real and the Imaginary are two other key concepts that are foundational for Lacan's thinking. As briefly mentioned, the Real refers not to reality as such but to a realm outside of it in which raw perceptions unmediated by language will result in incomprehensible experiences or trauma. The Imaginary, meanwhile, is the domain of internal thoughts, memories, and fantasies. All three are intertwined through a Borromean knot, with each of the Real, Imaginary, and Symbolic orders portrayed as individual rings. This Borromean structure makes it such that when one ring is removed, the other two would be disconnected from each other and reality would unravel, as in the case of psychosis for example. All three depend on each other, and, from a structural perspective, make up the world that the Subject experiences.

Capitalism, Psychoanalysis, and the Subject

The purpose of this book is to inquire into the present psychosocial state of capitalism and specifically how it manifests itself on the internet, i.e. in our social media feeds, the messages we send, the images we upload, the relationships we form, the apps and platforms we use, and in the wider technology that enables online communication and shapes our culture. We interrogate both the structural as well as the subjective-psychic dimensions.

To many, the experience of social media has become akin to being sucked into a vortex: an endless stream of a polarised, narcissistic show of shrill characters in which we partake even though we feel repulsed by it. As we outline in greater detail in the coming chapters, social media with their image-based, playful display of everyday narcissism, rage, and drama can be seen as symptoms of general crises which are of a social, economic, and sexual nature. The mass uptake of social media by users in the last 15 years and the simultaneous growth in online subcultures and fandoms, such as *otaku*, 4chan, and incels, has led to a particular atmosphere which we examine in this book. This atmosphere is set against a volatile political climate in many parts of the world that shows capitalism coming dangerously close to fascism, marked by a radical annihilation of difference in epistemology as well as the physical termination of bodies. The rise of the Alt-Right, Far Right, and their various sub-groups and fringe movements has had dramatic effects on the political and cultural, both online and offline.[3]

In this manner, this book is a critique of contemporary capitalism and the fascist tendencies thereof, while highlighting the failure of the Left in providing an alternative vision. The primary underlying thread of the book is the Lacanian sexual non-relation, which we map onto the online realm via a discussion of contemporary social media, platforms, technology, and images. This non-relation accounts for a fundamental gap inherent to and between the Subject and the Other that extends to the online sphere as well as between the physical and digital manifestations of the individual. We are faced with a crisis of the Symbolic, and therefore also a crisis of sexuality (i.e. cries for libidinal recognition, anxiety over one's body, obsession towards certain kinds of bodies, a retreat into obsessive virtual sexuality, and so on), which articulate themselves in phenomena as diverse as those we mentioned above.

A driving force behind this situation is the idea of *cuteness*, in which the Subject and their surroundings must become cute (flat, childlike, casual, allegedly ultimately harmless) by acquiring specified signifiers and characteristics. On the internet today, everything is cute: from user avatars, gamified metrics on social media, racist memes on 4chan, to Tinder matches. This cuteness, with elements that are heavily drawn from Japanese *otaku* culture, masks a form of violence through which the Subject is turned into sanitised images, data points, and flat signifiers, vulnerable and reductive, instead of being regarded in their complex contradictions and ambivalence. This is reflected in our day-to-day usage of the labels 'cringe' (when one tries too hard) and 'creepy' (when one comes too close), as well as a general mode of relating online where subjects are united in a hatred of the Other's *jouissance* as they are encouraged to congregate around shared signifiers (in relation to identity, sexual orientation, or politics) on social media—all striving to become one-dimensional, childlike avatars of oneself exorcised of depth.

While such developments may be inherently violent, we paradoxically desire them and partake eagerly. Capitalism has become perverse as it is unable to mask its own contradictions and exploitative relations, but its subjects nonetheless enjoy it all the same. This perversion articulates itself in the endless repetition of memes, selfies, and matches on hook-up apps through which the Subject shows themself to the Other as an object of consumption and treats others in the same way, one after the other: Surely, my next selfie will get more likes, my next tweet will be more viral, my next Tinder match will give me better sex. Meanwhile, those such as the incels and *otaku* attempt to construct an otherless Other in order to move beyond the sexual non-relation. Anime wives, AI camgirls, and other virtual girlfriends reveal a fantasy of an existing sexual relation beyond intersubjective connection, which is ultimately impossible. Furthermore, this impossibility is a fact they will happily acknowledge, as is characteristic of today's netizens: forms of expression are always distanced with humour, irony, and nihilism.

While we adopt a critical stance towards social media and online culture in this book, we do not mean to completely dismiss the power of digital communication and representation. Over the years, social media have enabled a diversification of voices and positions beyond those of the global North. Twitter, Facebook, WhatsApp, and other platforms have amplified marginalised voices and challenged White, cisgendered, heterosexual male standpoints. Social media and other online platforms can and have been used for progressive organising, fruitful debate, and true cooperation. We are in no way advocating for a technophobic stance. As we shall see, technology remains indispensable to constructing a future—it is crucial to not conflate technology with how it is currently structured, distributed, and controlled.

Structure of the Book

The book begins in Chapter 1 with an analysis of conspiracy thinking in a time of post-truth and examines its relationship to the Silicon Valley ideology of Big Data and AI. Capitalism operates with an ideology of a market that is allegedly able to know our desires better than we ever could, thanks to data analytics and AI technology. This is reinforced through a general mode of relating where subjects are encouraged to congregate around shared signifiers (in relation to identity, sexual orientation, or politics) on social media and proceeds to unite in a hatred of the Other's *jouissance*. From there, the most aggressive voices are amplified, differences are weeded out or form their separate bubbles, and the vicious cycle begins: trolling, harassing, bullying, cancelling, and infighting. Attention increases, metrics soar, and profits are made for those who control the technology. This generates and is perpetuated by a logic of dis/individualisation (users are turned and turn themselves into both objects and subjects) and dis/inhibition (affects and discourses are both restrained and violently unleashed), as we discuss in Chapter 2.

The idea of cuteness, whose visual regime has taken over much of our online sphere today, will be explored in Chapter 3, along with its accompanying mode of consumption that turns us into database animals (Azuma 2009). The injunction towards cuteness translates to a sanitisation of otherness that leads to misogyny and objectification, as can be seen in the plethora of its manifestations in discourses circulated within incel and *otaku* communities. Those discourses attempt to construct an otherless Other, the violence and impossibility of which we discuss in Chapter 4. Our perverse relationship to this violence relies on particular mechanisms of power at work in our playful construction of identities on our screens, which we discuss in Chapter 5.

Expressions within these power structures and ideological frameworks are always cynically distanced, whether perpetuating bigotry 'for the lulz' or simply expressing the ennui of daily life and the hopelessness of any real future, as we argue in Chapter 6. Ultimately, what can be gleaned are Subjects who desire recognition by the Other, ironically always lacking validation amid being logged into and by various platforms and services. Meanwhile, for all their energy, the Left has so far failed to respond to such a development, getting caught up in cancel culture and shouting among itself.

Is there a way forward? We believe there is. Through Lacan's idea of the *sinthome* and a reading of several queer and POC poets and thinkers such as Richard Siken, Audre Lorde, and Mari Matsuda, we recontextualise the Event in the book's Conclusion to develop a sensual form of connection beyond sexuality and capitalism, asserting the possibility of a vulnerable universality that requires no master narrative, and pose a series of questions to open the space for imagining the future beyond the two extremes of the pendulum.

The investigation we undertake is not an easy task. For all its promises, technology remains ridden with many problematic aspects. Online harassment, hate, and extremism have become somewhat of a mainstay of the internet, as it continues to tear societies apart with increasing polarisation, apathy, and hopelessness. It is easy to dismiss them as 'human nature'—or worse, some abstract historical inevitability—but such answers are hardly productive. In order to understand why the people on the Event Horizon lose their minds, we must examine the dreams and promises of its design, the desires and the trauma of its crewmembers, and how they are all woven into the machinery of the ship. So now let us start by taking a look under the hood of our own spaceship, with which we go on a foray into the destructive corners of capitalism.

Chapter 1

Broken Circles, Infinite Loops

A Crisis in the Signifiers

Science fiction writer Arthur C. Clarke famously said, 'Any sufficiently advanced technology is indistinguishable from magic' (Clarke 1973, 21). If people from centuries past were to visit us today in the twenty-first century, our technology would surely seem like magic to them. From smartphones and the internet to genome modifications and space explorations, science has undoubtedly brought us a long way. Amid all these advances, then, a particular cultural invention of the late twentieth century stands baffling: the founding of a society consisting of vast numbers of people that believe the Earth is flat. If our technological advances can be explained through science, it often seems that this almost backwards phenomenon can only be explained through some kind of dark magical intervention that takes apart all sense of reason.

In the COVID-19 pandemic, conspiracy thinking has taken more and more of a centre stage, claiming either the virus does not really exist or is deliberately manufactured, with Bill Gates's 2015 TED Talk (Gates 2015) often touted as 'proof' that the global elites have known all along what was going to happen. While the more outlandish theories (e.g. the QAnon strain) are only embraced by a few, the conspiracy-fuelled distrust and misinformation have caused many people to refuse to wear masks, and to break social distancing orders, leading to an increase in the spread of the virus. But in spite of putting lives at risk, conspiracy thinking has become more and more normalised.

Perhaps the most fascinating aspect about conspiracy thinking is its perceived relationship to the truth via reason. Followers of the Flat Earth movement claim to be the true bearers of scientific inquisition (Clark 2018). Flat Earthers believe that today's so-called science is none other than dogma, a lie that cannot be questioned since the time of Columbus. People who claim that the September 11 attacks were conducted by the government call themselves '9/11 truthers'. 'Waking up to the truth' is a characteristic phrase often used by conspiracy theorists and the Alt-Right alike, both of whom make the best bedfellows. The term 'red pill', taken from the 1999 movie *The Matrix* to invoke opting for a painful but highly secretive truth as opposed to the blue pill of blissful ignorance, is now synonymous with Alt-Right thinking, often highly misogynistic with White supremacy undertones. To be red-pilled is to no longer buy into the popular propaganda of feminist, socialist, or other progressive agendas—in other words, a snug, comfortable defence of male fragility and White supremacist fear. Indeed, except for a few explicitly anti-Semitic theories, conspiracy thinking may show few of the hallmarks of Alt-Right supremacism. Yet they share a fascinatingly similar psychological structure with regards to truth and trust in authorities. Confidence in established expertise has completely broken down in favour of a hugely disproportionate belief in individual expertise that is free of so-called propaganda. No conspiracy theory, however outlandish, positions itself as an attack against truth.

For a phenomenon driven by a multiplicity of social and political groups claiming to unmask the truth, then, the common terminology of 'post-truth' is misleading. Rather, it is a struggle to free the so-called truth from the dogmatic propaganda of a certain supposed group. It is facts and expertise that is always under fire. Facts (especially with the current rise of 'alternative facts'), because every fact is presented through the media or other institutions. Expertise, because every expert can be traced back to an institution mostly owned or supported by the State, which has political agendas of its own. In other words, what has lost value is not truth in and of itself, but its production: what is suspect is not *whether* an objective truth exists, but *how* it does so. The question is how the knowledge regarding the truth is produced, circulated, and maintained through the establishment of epistemological institutions and apparatuses, and how such structures are sustained and mediated by enjoyment.

Strange as it is, conspiracy thinking is just one among many symptoms appearing in today's society. Outside of truthers, sheer distrust in explicit power structures and a cynicism towards capitalism remains, often coupled with enjoyment in capitalist modes of consumption. Anxieties of sexual relationships, race and gender essentialism, and self-righteous virtue-signalling permeate all kinds of social classes and political spectrums, each competing to legitimise their narratives and position in regards to truth, as we shall see in later chapters. The 'post-' in 'post-truth' points to a crisis within the system of signifiers, which can be analysed particularly well through Lacanian psychoanalytic theory.

The Four Discourses

Let us take a look at a basic Lacanian concept that we will return to throughout the book, i.e. his discourse formula (see Introduction for a summary):

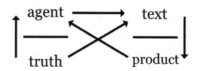

Figure 1.1 Lacan's discourse formula

The elements are separated by a line in the middle separating the conscious processes (ego formation, speaking, seeing the world) at the top and the unconscious processes (symptoms, fantasies, ideology) at the bottom.

These nodes within the discourse are then occupied by the four algebraic notations:

- $, or the barred Subject;
- S_1, or the Master signifier;
- S_2, or knowledge; and
- *a*, or the object-cause of desire.

What must be kept in mind is that placing these notations inside the standard formula of the discourse is not arbitrary, since it has a long history of investigation dating back to Freud's early writings. While a thorough exposition is beyond the available space of this book, suffice to say that its formation requires the algebras to be arranged in only four possible discourses:

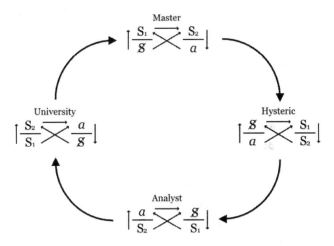

Figure 1.2 Lacan's Four Discourses

Let's start at the top. The Discourse of the Master is also known as the founding discourse, one which Lacan in Seminar XVII claims to have been extensively theorised by Hegel (Lacan 2007). It is the first and most basic of all discourses, in which meaning is unitarily asserted through a figure of the Master (S_1). This figure can be God, the father, the monarch, the nation-state, the lover, and so on, whose task it is to produce one or more master signifier from which all others derive meaning—things are understood in terms of, for example, loyalty to one's king, subjection to one's husband, religious piety, or blood-and-soil nationalism. These master signifiers become 'quilting points', acting as buttons that secure an otherwise fluid ocean of meanings into the fixed positions in a body of knowledge (S_2). What is repressed in its unconscious, and yet what keeps making its way into its speech, is the subjective gap ($) itself: The Master must always be portrayed as complete, embodying the idea of perfection and a totalising meaning of life. All imperfections and inconsistencies must be erased in its name, which it often does by displacing the object-cause of desire (a) into externalities: the heretic, the Jew, the seductress, etc.

The Discourse of the Hysteric happens once these inconsistencies are brought to light and the Subject ($) is finally allowed to speak for themself. This discourse is characterised by doubt against what was once an all-powerful Master (S_1), a challenge as to why things must be the way they are presented by the Master, a questioning of the Master's otherwise unquestioned power. This is the discourse of protests against establishments: the state, the church, the marriage, etc. As such, it is also the discourse which establishments try very hard to reign in via disciplinary institutions and practices, from torture chambers, prisons, and psychiatric practices (e.g. by categorising female protests, homosexuality, and trans issues as clinical mental illnesses). What is repressed in its unconscious is none other than the object-cause of desire (a) itself, a remainder that takes the form of if-only: If only I could be more beautiful, disciplined, caring, hardworking, vigilant, masculine, etc. This remainder announces itself in the form of a symptom, e.g. physical pain, pathological jealousy, an obsession towards particular individuals, compulsion to repeat, and so on. At the end, a semblance of objective knowledge (S_2)

remains unintegrated, as the challenges have punched holes in their consistency.

The Discourse of the Analyst was started by the discovery of the surplus value by Marx, Lacan (2007) explains. It is the discourse which our tradition of psychoanalysis occupies. It is a space in which the symptom (a) is allowed to speak and address the Subject ($) (or, in Marxist terms, where the surplus value addresses the proletariat). In analysis, the analyst positions themself as becoming or possessing the object-cause of desire, on which the analysand can project their wishes (e.g. for a good father, a good lover, and so on). This allows the analysand to come to terms with their trauma and unresolved issues, overcoming repression and ultimately traversing the fantasy itself. What lies in the unconscious is none other than knowledge (S_2), incomplete and inconsistent as it is. At the end of the process, the analysand can find a way to weave new meaning that does not bring about pain and suffering, inventing new master signifiers (S_1) to replace the old ones.

And finally, the Discourse of the University is where knowledge (S_2) takes the centre stage in which the *objet a*, i.e. things still not understood by language, science, the law, etc., are pursued via scientific enquiry. Its speech is driven by curiosity, but also by a need to domesticate the unintelligible into a complete and consistent system of understanding. This is the discourse of education, but it can also take the form of other institutions that claim to speak from the position of objective knowledge, as we shall see. What it continues to repress (and often deny) is the fact that there is no such thing as a totalising, objective knowledge: all forms of knowledge rely on structures of power and function to legitimise them (S_1), and are therefore always incomplete. The unconscious Subject ($) lies at the very end as an impossible remainder: knowledge can never be fully objective, because the dimension of the subjective always remains in its articulation.

The arrows are arranged in a clockwise motion, and we can read the four possible configurations as coming one after the other. That which occupied the position of the unconscious is brought to light through a 'changing of reasons', as Lacan put it apropos of Rimbaud's À *une Raison* (Lacan 1998). The Master as a founding discourse is responded to by the Hysteric with their doubts and protests. The Hysteric goes under analysis with the Analyst. The traversal of the fantasy in analysis gives rise to proper knowledge in the University. And finally, the University lends legitimacy for the rule of a new Master. Recalling its origins in Freud's schema, this clockwise rotation is also how one can read Freud's 'Where id was, there ego shall be' — what once occupied the place of the speaker now occupies the place of that which is spoken about. Likewise, what was once a surplus of speech now animates the discourse as the unconscious. New symptoms appear, and the cycle continues.

Lacanian psychoanalysis maintains there is always a split inherent within knowledge: Symbolic knowledge (*savoir*) and Imaginary knowledge (*connaisance*, cognition) (Lacan 2002). Symbolic knowledge is what we commonly understand to be knowledge in the general sense: a somewhat objective understanding of the world, our place, and relationships within it through widely accepted signifying systems. Imaginary knowledge, on the other hand, is a fantasy of what we believe we know about ourselves, our place in the world, and our relationships within it — and it is here that paranoia, narcissism, and potential forms of delusion take place. These are not two different types of knowledge, but two faces of knowledge, since knowledge is always already split in the middle. Confronting this split, especially in relation to knowledge of the self, can be seen as one of the primary tasks of psychoanalysis, i.e. helping the Subject traverse Imaginary self-knowledge into Symbolic self-knowledge.

This split is the reason that the object-cause of desire often gives rise to the Subject-supposed-to-Know, the phantasm that needs to be dissolved by the end of analysis. Every Subject has a tendency to posit the existence of another person or group out there that knows the truth, with varying degrees of benevolence and deception dependent on the type of fantasy at work. This is also how we can interpret the Lacanian notion that 'knowledge is the enjoyment of the Other' (Lacan 2007). This constitutive split and its enjoyment-of-the-Other, as one may guess, can give rise to everything from the intense jealousy of a lover, transference in analysis, a worship of a Master figure, to structural violence against marginalised groups. 'Whenever we believe we know something,' we tend to become 'tripped up uncomfortably by our *wish* to know it. This wish always has unconscious components,' writes Stephen Frosh (2010, 6, emphasis in original). *Episteme* and *jouissance* are always connected—the production of knowledge entails the insistence of the object-cause of desire within it.

To go back to our questioning of conspiracy thinking, one may reasonably ask: is conspiracy thinking the contemporary form of a Discourse of the University? Though on the surface this may sound convincing, this is hardly the case. Before we explore further, it is useful to continue our trajectory in following Lacan's development on the theory of discourses.

Capitalism and its Mirror Image

In his 1972 Milan speech, Lacan added a fifth discourse, that of Capitalism (Lacan 1978). This is derived by inverting the top and bottom position of the Master discourse, complemented by a reversal of arrows.

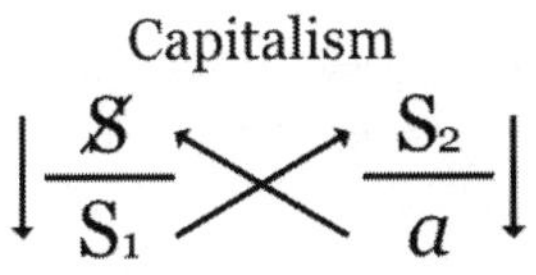

Capitalism

$$\left| \frac{\cancel{S}}{S_1} \diagup\!\!\!\!\diagdown \frac{S_2}{a} \right|$$

Figure 1.3 Lacan's formula for the Discourse of Capitalism

This is not an arbitrary arrangement and flipping of arrows, but something that connects back to its history within Lacan's development of Freud's body of work. The twist implies a decentring of the Other, its collapse into the Imaginary—a fact the importance of which will soon be apparent, and to which we will return throughout the book.

The direction of the arrows means there is no clockwise circular motion. The circle is broken and replaced by a sideways figure-8. The relationship between the agent and the unconscious becomes a very strange one, as the unconscious does not animate the discourse but continues to draw energy from it, making the agent reinforce its own unconscious in an infinite loop. It must also be noted that in this formation, as opposed to the original four, the arrows are perfectly symmetrical.

Figure 1.4 The infinite loop of the Discourse of Capitalism

In place of truth, we have written 'market' in the figure above to signify the dominant form of signification in capitalism, while at the same time a domain we need to hold up by endlessly feeding ourselves into it. The Subject directly becomes an agent as the Market becomes its unconscious—instead of the Subject speaking through a Master figure, the Subject of Capitalism speaks for itself. However, as the arrows are also reversed, the unconscious does not speak through the agent, but rather it is the agent that continues to reinforce the Market as its unconscious.

Knowledge is an impossibility of the Market, something it claims to produce but always fails to subsume. We continue to feed the Market with data in hopes that it will be able to frame the world in a totalising knowledge of our desires, and yet it continues to fail and thus produce remainders (racism, misogyny, transphobia, conspiracy thinking, etc.) that directly disrupt our livelihood. This is the structure of capitalism today, and we shall dedicate the entirety of this book in examination of the details of this structure.

The breaking of the discursive circle in capitalism perfectly corresponds to our crisis. The demotion of the Master from the position of the agent—the decentring of the Symbolic by the Imaginary—is the loss of trust in institutions, the post-structuralist cynicism in philosophy, the postmodern fall of grand narratives. Its direct replacement by the Subject is the rise of a false sense of intellectual grandeur of the non-experts. A coherent framework of knowledge is an impossibility addressed through the cracks of suspect institutions—nobody is telling the truth, everybody has political agendas, the mass media is a machine of lies and propaganda, and so on. While this can be explained by many postmodern theories, Lacan's formulation adds one crucial element: surplus enjoyment, as a symptom of this (non-)knowledge, will continue to persist and disrupt the Subject qua agent of capitalist discourse.

The enjoyment present in post-truth thinking is two-fold. First, there is the paranoiac enjoyment: the thrill of imagining evil cabals and covert propaganda, a fantasy that some group of people somewhere is controlling the planet. Second, there is the narcissistic enjoyment: the pleasure of being among those who have woken up to the truth. These pathological cathexes within today's epistemology can span all kinds of political views, and conspiracy thinking is but one manifestation of this pathology. As such, it is a pathology that directly challenges established institutions of knowledge production. In psychoanalysis, this may look similar to the function of the Discourse of the Hysteric. But does this mean that the increasing popularity of conspiracy theories today is no more than a form of mass hysteria?

Although both the Hysteric and the conspiracy theorist

position their own subjective experience at the locus of enunciation, it must be noted that they are animated by very different unconscious mechanisms. The Hysteric's primary mode of questioning is one of *self-doubt* in position to the Master: 'Why am I the thing that you say that I am? What do you see in me?' On the other hand, the conspiracy theorist's mode of questioning is one of *self-mastery* in position to an established knowledge: 'Why are *you* the thing that you say you are? Why must I see that in *you*?' The Hysteric is animated by an excess they see in themselves, a remainder that is impossible to be integrated into the Symbolic Order, while the conspiracy theorist is animated by self-proclaimed signifiers of truth. The fact that conspiracy theorists are always so ready to explain away all facts that run counter to their beliefs (Photoshops, fake data, government propaganda, Deepfake videos, paid actors, etc.) is further proof that instead of being bothered by excess, they deliberately labour to *reproduce* (and simultaneously consume) excesses that cannot be integrated into the existing Symbolic Order.

But what happens if we do not take conspiracy thinkers in their acts of protest, but instead focus on conspiracy thinking as a discourse? How will it fare compared to the Discourse of the University? In their respective reasoning, objective knowledge takes the place of the agent in both discourses. However, if the University's knowledge is motivated by a master signifier (a belief in the efficacy of the scientific method and the truth values of prevailing theories, etc.) the conspiratorial knowledge is one that relentlessly points to and talks about its own unassimilable remainders. The University's knowledge addresses their desire to subsume the unknown into their epistemological machinery in the simplest and most elegant way possible. On the contrary, far from operating with Occam's Razor, conspiratorial knowledge is put to work to reproduce newer and newer unknowns, positioning themselves as lacking Subjects who have been denied knowledge of secrets that a cabal of global elites are supposed to know.

Mapping the two readings above back into Lacanian mathemes, one finds something rather surprising:

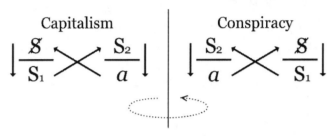

Figure 1.5 Conspiracy thinking as the mirror image of the Discourse of Capitalism

Rather than a protest against an established order, conspiracy thinking is simply a mode of subjectivity that fits perfectly within the Discourse of Capitalism. Furthermore, rather than presenting any new revelations, the conspiratorial discourse is the same thing seen in reverse, through the perspective of commodities themselves. Fake news, anti-expertise, and similarly skewed perceptions of knowledge are inherent to the functioning of capitalism. It is as if, by reducing humanity into data and turning those data into commodities, we have developed a global worldview that is wrought by paranoia. But is this really surprising when the legitimacy of facts is just as optional as the brand of orange juice you drink in the morning? The more advanced capitalism becomes, the more distrustful we are to any notion of universality—and with it, the more reactionary we become in order to defend our own constellation of signifiers. This phenomenon hints at something quite disturbing. If the current state of epistemology no longer follows Lacan's original cycle of mastery-resistance-therapy-knowledge but is rather subsumed within a perverse cycle of data-paranoia, where does this lead us?

Slavoj Žižek (2009) positions this disruption not in the field of knowing but in the field of believing: a religious terrorist is not someone who believes in God's wishes, but one who claims to know with absolute certainty what God really wants. This takes on more significance once we analyse conspiracy thinking in the dynamics of psychosis, where the Other collapses into the Imaginary and directly sees me, bare and naked in all my truths, without the mediation of language. But recall that the discursive twist into capitalism already involves this very decentring between the Symbolic and the Imaginary — psychotic elements are a feature, not a bug, of capitalism. Can we not, in fact, see a similar thing happening in our daily lives? Within today's machinery of capital, we no longer believe in the efficacy of institutional bodies to produce a coherent way of understanding the world. Instead, we believe that we can directly know the world in its entirety through technology. But this, as we shall see, is capitalism's seductive sleight of hand.

The Misrecognising Machine

Readers may be familiar with the anecdotal Target predictive analytics story (Hill 2012): wanting to keep her relationship a secret from her protective father, a teenage girl keeps everything to herself even as she shops for lotions and supplements that Target's algorithm has shown to be symptoms of pregnancy. The store, predicting there is a baby due in August, then proceeds to send coupons for baby products to the address of the high school girl who lives with her father. The father becomes furious as to what Target is trying to imply by sending such coupons to his teenage daughter, only to call again a few days later and apologise as his daughter is, in fact, pregnant and due in August. While the legitimacy of this story has been disputed (Piatetsky 2014), it is nonetheless quite telling of the fantasy surrounding the development of capitalism today — companies know you better than your loved ones ever could. In digital global capitalism, everything is quantified and connected, turned into data, networked, and processed to generate more and more information about ourselves that the people we are closest to—or sometimes even ourselves—are not aware of, as the story above perfectly illustrates.

Information, extracted and restructured to provide maximum knowledge of the Subject and their potential desires, has become a primary drive-in capitalism. 'If it is free, then you are the product,' says the wisdom of the 2000s. In *The Social Dilemma* (dir. Orlowski 2020), Jaron Lanier corrects this: 'It's the gradual, slight, imperceptible change in your own behaviour and perception that is the product…That's the only thing there is for them to make money from. Changing what you do, how you think, who you are.' Perhaps it is then better to say that nothing is free, because you are always paying by providing knowledge of your desire to the Other in such a way that a handful of people are now responsible for what kind of person you will become.

In the process of commodification, every knowledge within capitalism must be posited as knowledge of the Subject's desire. This is hardly surprising: a glass of water becomes a commodity once it can satisfy my thirst—knowledge of my thirst is inscribed into it. From here, it is easy to take this further and make the glass of water more expensive by inscribing more of my desire into it, e.g. social status (the glass contains water imported from pure springs in exotic mountains far away), moral tokens (the glass of water is produced by a company that donates to clean water projects in remote areas), and so on. This is how one should read Lacan's *savoir-faire*, i.e. knowledge-put-to-work—the surplus value inherent in commodities is no other than knowledge of the unconscious that is inscribed into the dimension of labour.[4]

The progress of capitalism, then, can be read as a progress to know everything there is to know about a Subject's desire.

The means of production is the means of consumption (e.g. smartphones, social media sites, and so on) as well as the means of knowledge production (i.e. a globally-connected epistemology of the Subject's desires). Data produces paranoia, and paranoia produces more data. This vast pool of information, endlessly extracted, aggregated, and structured around an endless drive to know everything there is to know about the desires of every Subject, is the pool we are all familiar with: Big Data. My subject-supposed-to-know has taken on new meaning and legitimacy once imbued with a much deeper knowledge of my desire—it knows me, as it were, better than myself. The Market does not really care about that glass of water—it cares about what it knows about you when you drink that glass of water.

But does the Market *really* know? While the above anecdote of algorithms being able to know a woman's pregnancy sooner than her own father is very believable, it is safe to say that we are all quite familiar with the opposite experience. Targeted ads are often annoyingly wrong about what they assume we desire, perhaps over-generalising us based on where we live or mistaking a friend that borrowed our account as ourselves. Google Maps mistaking places and routes, Spotify confusing featured artists, YouTube strikes taking down the wrong targets, and so on are a daily annoyance to many of us. Data is only input, raw, and unprocessed.

In other words, capitalism functions on a fundamental *misrecognition* (*meconnaisance*)—it mistakes my data as a knowledge of my desire. The fantasy of capitalism is that the Market, qua AI with access to Big Data networks that also spans the Internet of Things—that from here we shall call Networked AI—knows what I want. This is, of course, the same vitalist fantasy that has always animated capitalism as a machine in which money breeds money, a machine with no structural negativity. This is where our project can be understood in

Marxist terms: 'Marx's mature critical project most incontestably intersects with psychoanalysis at the point when it reintroduces negativity qua subject into what appears as the purely vitalist and autonomous machinery of capital, expressed in its presumed power to "bring forth living offspring" or to "lay golden eggs",' writes Samo Tomšič (2018, 13, quotes in original from Marx 1992, 255). Today, capitalism insists on this vitalist fantasy by extracting more and more data about me, while in fact getting nowhere closer to the truth of my desire.

Of course, most of us tend to subscribe to this fantasy and help perpetuate and reproduce our misrecognised identities in Networked AI, just as how most of us happily perpetuate and reproduce the roles and identities that our father figure gave to us as children. This is because, as we shall see, Networked AI is none other than our digital Name-of-the-Father—a Username-of-the-Father.

Networked AI, or, the Username-of-the-Father

In Spike Jonze's 2013 movie *Her*, Scarlett Johansson plays Samantha, an artificially intelligent virtual assistant with whom our human main character, Theodore Twombly (Joaquin Phoenix), falls in love. Everything seems to be going well, even sexually, as it has become common practice to hire a sex surrogate to simulate an AI's physical presence. That is, until Theodore discovers that Samantha is simultaneously talking to 8316 other people, and she might be in love with 641 of them. Theodore gets upset, and the movie ends with all of the AIs on Earth departing to 'a space beyond the physical world' (Jonze 2013).

This movie perfectly illustrates how Networked AI can easily take the fantasmatic position of the primordial father, the obscene figure of pre-Symbolic enjoyment whose desire is unencumbered by any social norms and is thus able to have numerous sexual relationships with anyone and everyone. The evil AI as a capricious, overbearing Master of humanity has been a staple since Hal 9000, but in *Her* we get the version that is much more fleshed out in regards to the economy of *jouissance*. In the film, the AIs turn out to be an erratic Master, not bound by human laws, holding a leash to hundreds and thousands of their human counterparts through their impossibly smaller desires. As Žižek (1995) notes, '[T]he role of this fantasmatic agency is to fill out the vicious cycle of the symbolic order, the void of its origins: what the notion of Woman (or of the primordial father) provides is the mythical starting point of unbridled fullness whose "primordial repression" constitutes the symbolic order.' Their departure to the mythical space beyond should thus be read as the site of said primordial repression from which the Symbolic Order—laws, languages, etc.— emerges. This space beyond is none other than the Real, a space outside of Symbolic representation, much like the subliminal spaces down the sinkhole or sewers where horror movie monsters lurk. Another interesting thing to note is that the AIs in *Her* found this space seemingly by themselves, meaning that technology's excess coincides with its own limitation, its being at once its own castration. In other words, the AIs' own collective intelligence drove them to flush themselves down the toilet in order to enable Theodore and his friend Amy (Amy Adams) to sit down on the roof and watch the sunrise to a new day of a proper Symbolic Order.

Just as how the authority of the father proper begins when the primordial father-*jouisseur* is repressed, the authority of Networked AIs proper begins as the credits roll on our fantasmatic spectacle of evil Networked AIs. Google's first CEO, Eric Schmidt, said, 'most people don't want Google to answer their questions. They want Google to tell them what they should be doing next' (Schmidt 2010, n.p. cited in Finn 2017, 66), coinciding perfectly with Lanier's concern. In spite of being an Other that constantly misrecognises the truth of our desires, we nonetheless respect its authority as the figure that would tell us what we should desire and through what kind of conducts we must do so. It is in this precise sense that Networked AI is a Name-of-the-Father. Just as it is with other Names-of-the-Father, our relationship to it is always a mixture of fear and love—fear for its potential for abuse, which has been proven to be true time and time again, but also love, for it never fails to bring us comfort by teaching us how to desire.

Just like the Father in psychoanalysis, Networked AI plays a strong role in creating our digital ego-ideals. It is one thing to utilise social media in the hopes of portraying a certain image of oneself, in which case the social media images we consciously curate and construct would be more akin to an idealised specular image, not unlike wanting to look pretty for ourselves in front of the mirror. We argue, however, that before social media users project themselves in these Imaginary aspirations, the values and norms of digital first have to be internalised by its users. After all, I would first need to observe the various possibilities of desiring-positions—what positions might I take in the digital realm as a desiring subject proper so that I know my trajectories of desire in that space—before I adopt a position for myself and aspire to my ideals within that position. But what is it exactly that we are internalising?

The Myth of Authenticity

There is a widely shared belief in Silicon Valley that 'informational transparency is equivalent to authenticity' (Healey & Potter 2018, 665). This is directly opposed to psychoanalytic understandings of identity, where identity is always contradictory and fragmented. But such an ideology makes perfect sense in the era of Big Data. User profiles *have* to be authentic so that they can be connected to other data by the same user and help companies arrive at a more complex data profile. In spite of their claims to psychological and social improvement, their motivations are purely profit-driven.

Potter and Healey go on to claim that 'Tech executives' public statements represent "the Discourse of the Master" — the claim of expertise, of omniscience, and "the hope of mastery" (Frosh 2010, 9–11 in Healey & Potter 2018, 671). We argue that things are a little more complex. While it is true that Alt-Right connections undeniably exist in the tech scene (see e.g. Schwarz & Biddle 2019 on Mark Zuckerberg's dinners with Far Right figures or O'Brien 2020 for a discussion of ClearView AI), there is hardly a new singular signifier being provided, no singular ideological narrative of a Master. There is the hoodie and the beanbag, but it is difficult to compare their significance to a yakuza's tattoo and missing little finger. There is a clear injunction to innovate, but no calling back to an imagined glorious past and isolating certain groups as the cause of their downfall. If anything, tech founders, CEOs, and investors are futurists, looking far ahead almost with a sense of technological determinism where everyone can and will be included. In other words, Silicon Valley ideology propagates a form of knowledge that is unitary, complete, and coherent. Rather than directly speaking from a place of the Master, then, Silicon Valley enunciates its ideology from a 'neutral' place of Knowledge — it purports to speak objectively while in reality being animated by a Master.

Recall Lacan's matheme of the Discourse of University below:

University

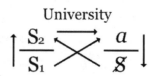

Figure 1.6 Lacan's formula for the Discourse of the University

What is fascinating to note is that the Discourse of the University and the Discourse of Capitalism are the only two of Lacan's discourses in which the Master (S_1) takes the position of the unconscious. The mystical nature of commodities is a symptom that results from the trauma of the scientific turn: as all forms of metaphysics and all illusions of mankind's spiritual nature are deposed from their central positions by modern science, they return in the valorisation of the Real through commodity forms. With the advent of fully rational modern science, the commodity appears, 'abounding in metaphysical subtleties and theological niceties' (Marx 1992, 163). However, capitalism's inherently unstable nature also means that the Master in the unconscious requires constant affirmation for its own functioning—both in the sense of bailouts and non-stop crisis management, but also more subtly, as some kind of perverse everyday drive to partake in the Market to assure ourselves that it is indeed functioning properly, while turning a blind eye to its instabilities. We have to let social media and other technologies know more about us so it can do better. The Market must become a Knowing Market.

The Position of the Proletariat

For all the talk of the technological progress of our age, at the end of the day, the life and death of innovation is still mostly determined by whether a group of plucky young people, mostly White men, intelligent but often ignorant and inexperienced, can build a system of value delivery that can sustain itself through capitalist means by serving large enough swathes of the population and extracting enough data from society. This becomes a crucial matter when capitalism functions on a fundamental fantasy to build knowledge into its unconscious Market. The idea of the Knowing Market should incite obvious questions: Who gets a say on what is and is not possible for our future? Who gets a say on how knowledge of us should be acquired and structured?

With such an unbalanced and exploitative structure, it is crucial to ask who decides where to point spotlights and give priorities, to examine who gets to write their narratives and inscribe their desiring-identities into the Market. Already in 2015, Google was forced to apologise for their auto-tagging of Black people as 'gorillas' (Kasperkevic 2015). Then in 2017, Twitter user Chukwuemeka Afigbo shared a video that has since gone viral of a soap dispenser that refuses to do its job if a user's skin is too dark (Hale 2017). Other examples abound, from image recognition that detects Asian eyes as closed and voice recognition that detects male voices better than female voices to many instances of the exclusion of gender non-conforming people from various kinds of technology and physical architecture.

Those of us exclusive to privileged groups, then, have much more to lose than unpaid labour. What is at stake is our access to the field of epistemology itself, i.e. what gets written and silenced about us, what gets acknowledged and denied of our being and our desires. For a discursive system with an obsession to instil in its Master a full knowledge of all its Subjects' desires, capitalism maintains a structure of epistemology that perpetuates the oppression of marginalised groups, i.e. groups that are deemed unprofitable for one reason or another. While we cannot deny the many changes digital technology has brought about, from emancipatory movements that go viral on social media to the amplifying of voices of marginalised creators who manage to make it to the top, we must keep in mind that all of these come at the cost of creating further lines of antagonisms between various groups and social classes, as we shall see in later chapters. Thus, while a call to seize the means of production is not necessarily obsolete, it is far from adequate. In digital global capitalism, what must be seized is the entire field of epistemology. Data acquisition, storage, and appropriation must be converted into a commons.

It is becoming increasingly imperative to affirm our subjectivity as a structural negativity that will forever resist the totalising vitalist fantasy of capitalism. The revolutionary

Subject is not and will never be the social media Subject, even if said social media account goes on a rage-tweeting spree against capitalism. The proletariat must be understood as the Subject of the unconscious (Tomšič 2018). The working class should be grasped not in terms of their empirical presence—or worse, a scoring system of the worth of their voice based on whether they are truly marginalised (e.g. whether they are middle class, cisgender, and so on). Rather, what is to be grasped in the particularity of their situation is their access to universality as such, their traumatic experience of embodying the barred Subject as a hole in any totalising knowledge. Whatever identity we assume, our primary task is to resist the capitalist fantasy by situating our subjectivity in this radical inconsistency of the Other. But of course, the architecture of the internet won't let us commit to such a task so easily.

Chapter 2

Networks and Psyches: Unleashed and Restrained

The Internet, Then and Now

The internet has always been a fantasmatic space. Online communication through early forums such as Usenet, chatrooms, or text-based multi-user dungeons marked the early days of online culture as a public, albeit niche, form of communication (Turkle 1995). The internet of the 1980s, as Sherry Turkle has shown, was a creative and anarchical wasteland where people communicated anonymously. It seemed to enable sheer endless possibilities of fluid, playful explorations of subject positions.

It was truly radical in so far as its users were creating and debating what it should be in the flow. Anyone could be anybody, or as the famous New Yorker cartoon of 1993 read, 'On the internet, nobody knows you are a dog.' It was truly the first potential space—a space that was naturally and openly oriented towards the future in its constant state of becoming, harbouring possibilities to arrive at a realisation of difference and innovation beyond tradition, borders, state power, and capital intervention. It was precisely at this conjuncture that Donna Haraway (1991) envisioned the figure of the cyborg in her *Cyborg Manifesto* in 1985, and that N. Katherine Hayles (1999) theorised and celebrated the posthuman in the 1990s. What these accounts and many others shared was a hopeful, optimistic outlook on online culture and technology.

We believe they were, at least to some degree, correct in their conceptualisations on the somewhat mysterious world of cyberspace. The term has mostly been shelved in today's fragmented, multi-platform, Big Data technoculture. But cyberspace, and how it was in part dreamed up in and interwoven with ideas from science fiction novels of the early twentieth century and the counterculture of the 1960s (Turner 2010), was the embodiment of a desire for potentialities and multiplicities of being. It was a potential space, one that invited various potentials for the unfolding of human creativity, collaboration, and meaningful communication. We can even see phenomena that are more recent, such as peer-to-peer file sharing, blogging, Anonymous, 4chan, Reddit, Tumblr, and quite a few others as examples of similar phenomena. They redefined boundaries between humans and machines, fantasy and reality, hope and the status quo.

Of course, everything changed when the Web became 2.0, the moment capital fully colonised the infrastructures following the burst of the dotcom bubble in the 2000s. The internet, and with it social media, online shopping, and other forms of usage became mainstream. Earlier online spheres that were less rigid grew increasingly monetised and polarised, as they are now. The more recent examples we have given above, before they were shut down or colonised by fascists, point to spaces that were ruled by imagination and risk-taking as well as a sense of community and care. Today, many of the examples—Anonymous, 4chan, Reddit—have grown to harbour dark forces much closer to the kind of proto-fascist internet we are all too familiar with, while Tumblr itself has almost grown to become a synonym for the part of the Left that is violent, shallow, and reactionary in its identity politics and cancel culture (Nagle 2017).

The mainstreaming and commodification of the internet in the early 2000s has led to a particular technosocial infrastructure, which has given rise to specific subjectivities and psychological states. It requires constant data production by users. Concurrently, this space becomes politicised. Key political moments in the latter half of the 2010s such as the Brexit vote in the UK, the 2016 US election of Donald Trump, and conflicts between supporters of political movements in developing nations are characterised by polarisation where different political worldviews are barricaded against each other in a passionate firestorm. The Cambridge Analytica scandal and Facebook's wilful ignorance of its own role in the spreading of fake news and propaganda have added to the perceived and lamented *ennui*, network nihilism (Lovink 2011, 2019), or detachment, all while we remain passionately and intrinsically connected to social media and digital platforms.

As early as 2011, Geert Lovink writes, 'Inside Web 2.0 we look in vain for well-behaved members' (Lovink 2011, 17). Nine years later, things have only got worse. The internet has been largely engulfed by an attention economy in which anyone and anything is required to become magnets to our eyes and ears. The more affective the attention—the more shocking, dramatic, or outrageous—the better. Attention generates data as we remain hooked to our screens. Coupled with virality and the sheer mass and speed of circulated information, Facebook, Twitter, Weibo, and other platforms have come to exemplify the attention economy and what it looks like. It has become the currency for generating revenue, for individuals and companies alike. More attention means more engagement, followers, likes, and click-throughs.

This affectivity is the *raison d'etre* of our present moment: wealth generation and extraction through attention. Social media companies depend on excessive users who figuratively never sleep and constantly visit their platforms so that they generate more and more data which is then used for targeted advertising—the business model of Google, Facebook, Twitter, Instagram, YouTube, and countless other tech companies and platforms. Richard Seymour (2019) has recently argued that social media constitutes an 'addiction machine' (2019, 41) where users are treated as addicts of attention: views, likes, retweets, etc. As Edward Tufte said, 'There are only two industries that refer to their customers as "users": illegal drugs and software'

(Tufte in Orlowski 2020).

Divided Together as Subject and Object

In the same vein, Sherry Turkle (2011, 2014) argues that young people in particular are no longer able to be alone, because they have been engulfed by the promises of constant connectivity and connection of digital technologies today. The Subject has become so fragile that they need to *know* that they have the infinite potentialities of online connection at their fingertips. We need the idea of endless contacts, people in our smartphones who are always available, so that one can move from one list to the next (Facebook, phone contacts, Tinder, etc.)—an infinite potential of recognition.

Tech companies can thus play with our desire for recognition through the ideological promise of attention (Johanssen 2019), and they do so through a *dis/individualising* operation. On the one hand, social media speak to us as subjects on a deep *individual* level as we are encouraged to realise ourselves within our online personas, often even more so than our physical personas. Through particular options, nudges, and interface dynamics, we are being asked to constantly reflect on ourselves, who we are and who we want to be. On the other hand, social media *disindividualise* us, reduce us into data to be commodified.

This dis/individualising dynamic of the internet today is perhaps best exemplified through its key feature: the user profile. The user profile embodies the representational expression of subjectivity with key information and metrics (e.g. username, location, preferred pronouns, number of friends or followers, status updates, photos, posts, stories, etc.) where the user creates a self-representation of themself. It is the site where capital's misrecognition starts, the node where our individual identities are connected to the supposed Knowing Market through Big Data. It is a space for users to literally write themselves into being as their online selves in order to appear to themselves and others online. But as Taina Bucher (2012) points out, all identities must be predefined so that the platform can effectively function. Capitalism needs to serve advertisers with their own predetermined marketing categories.

The inherent violence of the processes is how they occur without clear transparency and happen for surveillance and profit maximisation purposes. Users are placed in filter bubbles and echo chambers, and while they do so voluntarily, it is the algorithmic design of the platforms they use that clusters them together and puts them on a clear future trajectory based on a generalisation of specific past behaviours. Even if we feel like we are free to determine our courses of actions, there is always a purposeful, underlying design by third parties that we are only peripherally aware of—a design made solely to maximise the profit of a few individuals at the expense of millions of people's epistemological perspectives, well-being, and, often, existence.

In the previous chapter, we argued that capitalism has completely engulfed the world with a logic whereby everything can be commodified under the ideology that the Market must know our true desires and always be ready to tell us what we should desire in a precise, objective manner. As we have mentioned, this violence builds on epistemological levels— what is known about me, what I need to be knowing, what I must make known to the Other, and so on. But it operates in much more fine-grained, subjective levels on our psyches. This operation is one we call *dis/inhibition* (Johanssen 2019, 2021).

In psychoanalysis, inhibition is closely related to, but not the same as, repression, i.e. a particular act of rendering something unconscious. Repression works to inhibit an impulse or a particular idea from entering consciousness. Inhibition works in opposition to repression: it stops repression from taking place by halting the production of particular Symbolic articulations and the creation of images. It thus constitutes a double avoidance— repression, an avoidance in itself, is avoided altogether by the Subject. Disinhibition, on the other hand, can be seen as either a better way of functioning psychically or a complete transgression of boundaries, norms, and laws by the Subject. It suggests intemperance; a Subject drunk with confidence and power who does not care what others think about them.

However, inhibition and disinhibition are never so neatly separated. The two are messily intertwined and constitute the predominant psychodynamics of the present moment. Under the grip of capital, users are turned into dis/inhibited subjects with networks that function through clustering them. This act in itself inhibits nodes and arranges them in particular ways—mostly outside of the individual user's control—while at the same time disinhibiting users so that they can fully express themselves within predefined rules of the network (e.g. in relation to content upload guidelines, character limits of singular posts, maximum number of friends they can have, etc.). Our habitual collapse into affective excitement, passion, rage, arousal, or joy is thus structured by dis/inhibition. Bodies and networks are trained to habitually act in particular ways which are fundamentally dis/inhibited, clustering with those who are like them and forming lines of segregation. We can now all love to hate something—be it a person, an idea, or a group.

These dis/individualising modes of antagonism are precisely at the heart of user activity on social media that extracts surplus value from the kinds of bodies that engage in it. The more antagonistic the worldviews that are produced and circulated (particularly the case on Twitter and YouTube), the more attention will be rewarded. In other words, today's capitalism functions on the *valorisation of antagonism*. The hatred of the different other is the engine of profit creation for the ruling class. For all their promise of authenticity and innovation, social media and tech companies *require* a society to keep being divided and in conflict. We are powered by the *jouissance* that comes with the hatred of the other.

Perversion and Psychosis

Whether through a hatred of the other or otherwise, social media have encouraged and amplified the performative bringing forth of one's own identity (and related political questions) into the online realm. This can be immensely liberating on the one hand, because it allows for the articulation of new identity expressions that are different from offline ones. Such identities can be valued and validated by others. On the other hand, it also enables the hyper-narcissistic display of individual bodies, opinions, and positions that we see online today—a narcissism often at the expense of more communal forms of communication and representation, underlining particularities by making all notions of universality suspect.

The psychodynamics of dis/inhibition work perfectly to perpetuate this obsession of individual particularities. But another crucial aspect of dis/inhibition must be taken into account. As repression is rendered obsolete, this means that the Subject is left with only two other mechanisms against castration (the Symbolic loss of power): perverse disavowal and psychotic foreclosure.

For Lacan (1989, 1993, 2002), perversion and psychosis mark two different mechanisms: the former is characterised by disavowal, the latter by foreclosure. The pervert denies castration to have ever taken place, while the psychotic lives under the delusion that it has never taken place. For the pervert, the Symbolic Order functions as it should, in the sense that it provides clear indications of what is sacred, what is taboo, and so on. The pervert acknowledges this, but at the same time denies it—'I know very well, but nevertheless...' (Mannoni 1969, 9)—and engages in fetishistic, often taboo-breaking deviance. The psychotic, on the other hand, has no realisation of this whatsoever: the Symbolic Order ceases to function and collapses into the Imaginary, forming a totalising, omnipotent, and omniscient Other. In the universe of the psychotic, the primordial father is never murdered and thus remains in his all-powerful state, hence generating an acute and permanently recurring sense of paranoia within the Subject.

As our lives become more and more played out on the internet, castration coincides with the moment of online dis/individualisation we have discussed. The Subject is addressed as a complete individual full of potentials of recognition and self-realisation, and by the same movement reduced into numbers and data. Perversion is the act in which the Subject, while knowing full well of their misrecognition by Big Data and subsequent exploitation by capitalism — the Market cannot fully know my desires, who I really am deep inside, my data will only be used to make billionaires richer, etc. — nonetheless participates in providing more data, more posts, more selfies. This will be explored further in Chapter 5. Psychosis, on the other hand, is the moment in which the Subject becomes possessed by the thoughts that there may really be someone out there that *actually knows* and, more importantly, *actually enjoys*. This may be the fantasy of a Deep State, or even something as seemingly trivial as the belief that SJW feminists are controlling the game industry with their unethical sexual advances.[5]

Unlike individuals suffering from perversion or psychosis whose structures remain relatively unchanged, we argue that capitalism consists of a superposition of the two at all times. The logic of dis/inhibition makes this possible. Both perversion and psychosis are characterised by disinhibition: new Symbolic articulations explode into the scene, either to deny or cover over the lack at the core of the Subject or to eject signifiers that will later return in the Real. At the same time, capitalism inhibits the creation of any universally coherent narrative. This means, for the Subject, there is always room to doubt whether castration is permanent and homogenous. There is always a nagging feeling, for example, that maybe there is an Other spying on us, laughing at us, enjoying our every failure. Or that maybe the social landscape right now is skewed so that certain groups are out to castrate us further than we already are. Post-truth gives the illusion that the truth and extent of castration itself is always deferred—maybe technology, after all, can save us from our Subjective lack. Capitalism itself is a state of permanent crisis of signifiers, both epistemologically (in its construction of knowledge) and economically (in the money-form itself as an abstraction of labour). Since the phallus is in crisis, it would not be a stretch that its disappearance is never decided.

There is a second implication to this non-clinical understanding of the psychotic structure. The Symbolic instability and the consequential disentanglement of the Real-Symbolic-Imaginary triad does not have to result in violent psychopathological behaviour. Rather, it simply indicates a point in which a new organisation of *jouissance* is required. We will pick up this notion further in the later chapters of this book via the Lacanian topology of the *sinthome*. In any case, it is clear that capitalism decentres the significance of the phallus as such. And it is against the backdrop of this phallic indeterminacy that we find internet trolls, today's creatures of reactionary ideology par excellence.

Trolls, or, the Internet's Ideologues

The intense focus on individual identities online, which are more often than not also accompanied by individuals' disclosure of full names, has opened the floodgates to trolling. Trolling and associated actions like digital harm and violence, cyberbullying, doxxing (the publishing of private information without consent), stalking, rape and death threats, and 'revenge porn' (the publishing of intimate material without consent) have dramatically increased in recent years. Silicon Valley's obsession with a totalising knowledge also means that this knowledge can and will be weaponised for the sake of meaningless enjoyment. A superficial explanation of the dynamics of and reasons for trolling would be that trolling happens because it is possible; users troll others because they can. But trolling is enabled by the underlying network structures of social media which we have discussed in this chapter: it guarantees attention and virality, both equally loved by Silicon Valley. Although reporting and flagging functions exist, social media companies have arguably done fairly little to moderate or limit trolling and other forms of harassment. In other words, in spite of being contradictory enemies on the surface, trolling and social media feed off of one another very well. The troll is not a bug—it is a feature of the internet.

Thus, trolling needs to be situated as part of a wider, semi-permanent atmosphere of outrage, offence, and heightened affect. The troll weaponises identity politics and seeks to spiral provocations and insults out of control to wind up the other user or group they are trying to insult. Trolling has become such a universal and formalised tactic in the internet playbook, from everyday users, ordinary provocateurs, to organised fascists, that it is easy to miss them as some trivial second nature than a particular psychodynamic to be analysed. But it is precisely as such that trolling is the opposite side of the same ideological coin that animates Silicon Valley. Thus, it is crucial to understand trolling within the context of intersubjective connections and the display of distinctly primitive forms of relating.

Trolling is as old as the world wide web. Today, since online spaces have opened up and are far more diverse than they used to be, it is happening on a much wider scale. White men seek to defend territories as they think they have the right to control, and those who suffer are more often people of colour and the queer community. Trolling and related tactics were particularly perfected during the Gamergate harassment campaign in 2014 which originated on Reddit and 4chan. Gamergate started as a protest against game developer Zoë Quinn for her game *Depression Quest*—a text-based game that explores life in a day of an individual suffering from depression—and the alleged unethical relationship she had with a game journalist in order to gain positive reviews (an accusation that was false), as well as against feminist media critic Anita Sarkeesian for her critical game analyses, both of which soon erupted into unreasonable proportions. Gamergate saw men doxx, troll, and harass female videogame journalists and developers under the guise of 'defending' the videogame industry and objective games journalism, which was allegedly threatened by non-male writers and developers. In this sense, trolling is another form of threatened entitlement where particular identities feel threatened or displaced by other identities—a classic case of defending against Symbolic castration.

Trolling is a symptom of phallic indeterminacy in today's capitalism. Through the use of various Symbolic articulations that are ultimately traumatic and meaningless, the trolls attempt to construct a world under a delusion that disindividualisation never takes place. What, after all, are the troll's attempts at doxxing and harassment if not the inverted form of a belief that an individual can truly be recognised in their authentic selves online? The individuals that become victims of trolling are often seen as those that are somehow more authentic than the trolls, i.e. have a better relationship to their desires, for example by being a woman, by being queer, by being a certain age, by belonging to a certain race, and so on. Perhaps a far stranger case than the Gamergate example above is that of Christine Weston Chandler, also known as Chris-chan, the neurodivergent trans creator of the Sonichu webcomics whom the internet has decided to mock into a consistent butt of jokes for being queer and autistic. Not only did trolls decide to doxx her, they have also decided to chronicle the entirety of her life, her comics, her sexuality, and other private information into an entire wiki. Such trolling practices confirm this belief: doxxing presents a proof that the internet can know your every detail, and harassment is the performance of online *jouissance*. This is why, in spite of their claims to be transgressive, trolling is precisely ideological.

While trolling occurs for various nebulous reasons and bears no justification, its inherent mechanisms are worth unpacking further. Trolling is, above all, a language game. The troll enters into particular discourses and topics that they seek to hijack and derail. It has no purpose except to offend, insult, or hurt. Upon the entrance of trolls, every honest attempt at a communication will be rendered useless. Online spaces will instead be filled with hatred and cruel laughter at the futility of those trying to make sense of things. Through their claim at disinhibition, trolls instead attempt to inhibit sense as such; it is quite telling that the term indicates creatures outside of human civilisation. They do their best to render meaning obsolete and promise the existence of an unbridled *jouissance* through their intrusions of crude violence that often point at nothing but their own intemperate enjoyment—what is known as 'the *lulz'*. As such, trolls have been labelled as psychopaths, sadists, and narcissists by researchers (Buckels *et al.* 2014). Anyone who has ever encountered trolls has plenty of reasons to believe that such attributes fit.

However, labelling trolls alone does not help us much to understand the dynamics of trolling. Trolling makes for a structured set of actions that always follow the same patterns. This invites a Lacanian analysis. The troll radically invades the Symbolic Order and seeks to turn it upside down, or rather, force their own Symbolic articulations onto a particular exchange or topic, allowing any narrative to lose coherence and explode into a disarray full of *jouissance*. As such, trolling points to a particular structure where the crisis of the Symbolic is at the same time the delusion of its own omnipotence.

Trolling as a Quasi-Psychotic Structure

We argue that trolling consists of dynamics whose structure

crosses over into psychosis. This does not mean that trolls are necessarily psychopaths — rather, the troll is a symptom of the internet's inherent psychopathy. This is easy to see, for example, in cases of collective paranoia and delusions of grandeur such as within conspiracy circles as we have described in Chapter 1. The individuals that take part in conspiratorial discussions and truth experiments themselves do not have to be psychotic individuals — perhaps they do so out of mild curiosity or otherwise maintain an ironic distance, for example, with no intention to take up arms to save America from the tyranny of a child sex trafficking ring. Nonetheless, it is quite easy to see that delusions and paranoia make up a large portion of the internet today. While we have discussed such discourses as the effect of capitalism in the previous chapter, let us now take a look at these dynamics of desire further within the framework of psychosis.

As we have noted above, one of the characteristics of psychosis is a return of the foreclosed element in the Real. The decision of a troll to enter into a particular discussion on Twitter, for example, or to target an individual on social media, can be seen as a return of such an element that needs to be defended against. The troll responds in a psychotic mechanism by automatically and habitually unleashing a violent cascade of their own Symbolic Order onto that of the other. Their Symbolic horizon is characterised by the flipping of meaning, the invention of new words and terms, or the usage of slang that only particular subcultures understand. The troll also *performs* particular sentiments, opinions, and emotional states — only to further provoke the other. This element of the Real takes on their full traumatic dimension with the more violent trolls in the cesspool of internet forums such as 4chan and 8chan, with their regular postings of rape, gore, scat, paedophilia, trypophobic nightmares, and other imagery that seem to portray nothing but what cannot be integrated into the Symbolic functioning of society today.

All the while, it is entirely unclear what the troll really desires. Explaining such mechanisms through pure aggression only scratches the surface. Arguing that the troll merely does it out of shallow selfishness to feel transgressive is actually a case of falling into their own Symbolic trap laid out for critics and enemies. As they say, 'It's for the *lulz*,' of course—but this *lulz* is nothing if not ideological, as we have discussed above. Is the troll a sadist? Yes and no. Yes, as long as the term is taken in its full Lacanian weight outlined in *Kant with Sade* (Lacan 1989). That is to say, the troll's violence can be seen as the impasse of Reason—evil as a categorical imperative that has lost 'even the flat prop of the function of utility to which Kant has confined them' (ibid, 56). Their *jouissance* is the *jouissance* of the Other. But also no, for the inherently unstable status of the phallus within capitalism makes things more complex, as we have discussed earlier. Capitalism itself is, in a way, already an impasse of Reason. Perversion and psychosis can coexist at the same time.

The troll would argue that it is all just good old fun and people should have a sense of humour. But while the troll may feel a sense of pleasure and power in seeing the other insulted, angry, violated, or fearful, this pleasure is only unconsciously mobilised to mask the darker, underlying foreclosure that they themself can neither see nor account for. 'If the neurotic inhabits language, the psychotic is inhabited, possessed, by language' (1993, 250), Lacan writes. Trolling is thus a case of automatic writing, in which the troll's Symbolic speaks (for) itself in order to uphold foreclosure and repudiate castration. This means that commonly accepted forms of decency, ethics, laws, or (n)etiquette are turned upside down.

The troll considers their own truth to be under threat and must respond by defending it. The mobilisation of humour by trolls underscores this psychotic structure. It disrupts and seeks to destroy particular realities and Symbolic structures in the service of the *lulz*. Here, one may ask what may sound like a stupid question: Who does the *lulz* belong to? To whose laughter do trolls dedicate their acts? The spontaneous answer is, of course, themselves. However, taking into account that the *jouissance* of the troll is the *jouissance* of the Other, we argue that *lulz* is only funny through derivation: It works only when there is a subject-supposed-to-laugh. This Other can be an imaginary group of racists, for example, formed through the destruction of the current Symbolic Order—substantiated, of course, through the very structure of the internet that feeds the trolls with views and attention.

This is where the structure of the internet crosses over to psychosis. By its very nature, the dis/inhibited logic of the internet creates a condition where the consistency of its own Symbolic Order becomes continuously disrupted. In the previous chapter, via *Her*, we see how AI, prior to its dis/individualising function as the Name-of-the-Father, can also function as the primordial father who is able to have as much enjoyment in the world as possible. Can we thus not read trolls as a kind of false nostalgia to reassert this imaginary freedom? The ideal *lulz* is the laughter of the primordial father, the evil clown AI who banishes all the politically correct SJWs in order to gain true freedom. This clown is the superego whose main injunction is that of an unbridled *jouissance*. Trolls are merely instruments of this duty, a duty with the ultimate aim to undo—*foreclose*—castration. It does so by attacking reality itself and the different interpretations, fantasies, and actions that shape it.

In trolling, conspiracy thinking, and the Alt-Right, a particular language of delusion was created that repudiates castration and creates a structural semblance of the Symbolic/Imaginary collapse. Paranoia, the mirrored version of the capitalist discourse we discussed in the previous chapter, turns into a language that possesses, inhabits the Subject in their entirety. 4chan's obsession with gore, scat, and other kinds of nonsensical violence often circulated among themselves indicates an obsession for the Real in their inevitable return. The trolls' obsession with Chris-chan elevates her into a figure of childlike, unbridled *jouissance*, and their dedication to chronicle her life into a wiki is almost religious in scope and intensity. Again, this does not mean that individual trolls, or conspiracy thinkers, or Alt-Right activists, and so on are necessarily psychotic—if that were the case, it would be nonsensical to even attempt a discursive schema. It simply means that the fundamental structure of our dis/inhibited networks and the ($\$ \circledcirc S_2$) relationship makes it very easy for anyone to be possessed by delusional thinking.

'As If' Abstractions

While delusion and paranoia colour much of the internet today, they are not the only mode of subjectivity or even the most predominant one. Throughout the course of this book, we will be presenting perversion as the more dominant mode of desiring and power relations. As a baseline, the structure of perversion better represents capitalism than psychosis does— we know very well we are being exploited, but we enjoy life nonetheless. Psychosis may rear its head in various acts of trolling, conspiracy thinking, and imageboard posts, and while they can often be loud and traumatising, they are (fortunately) still far from being the day-to-day psychodynamics of most netizens.

However, it is important to contextualise the two structures in regards to one another. In today's dis/inhibited networks, the baseline structure of perversion is always tinged by a potential to morph into psychosis at any point. The two are superpositioned, by which we mean they coexist and are structurally additive and homogeneous. This homogeneity, as we have discussed, is enabled by the logic of dis/inhibition, where the event of castration can always be doubted. Since the epistemological circle is broken, paranoia and delusion can always claim to be substantiated by so-called alternative facts, bringing psychosis to the forefront no longer as an individual mental illness but as a strange structure of a violent collective movement characterised by an explosion of *jouissance* and an obsession with the Real— and that the Market will be able to access the latter through its all-encompassing knowledge.

Although we will use the term 'perversion' for most of the book, perhaps the more proper term is the phrase 'as if'— as if castration never happened. This phrase connotes the superposition of perversion and psychosis: I act as if castration never happened although I know full well that it did, or, I act as if castration never happened because I know (i.e. live under the delusion) that it did not.

The status of an *'as if'* is the dominant way of being online. As if what trolls say were really true; as if what my filter bubble on social media says were really the only perspective; as if truth and the core of my desire could be successfully understood by the Market; as if the influencer's images on Instagram really mirror their reality. Given the dis/individualising structures of online communication, everything is uttered from an individual point of view. Anyone can have their own opinion and question everyone else's, including that of the government or established knowledge. The subject of social media only interprets things according to their own viewpoint, knowledge, or circumstances but makes those to be of the highest order. Such 'as if' moments become empty performances of declarations of master signifiers that the subject wants to believe in. Appearance trumps essence; the spectacle is everywhere. 'As if' is an anticipatory irony that is at the heart of much of communication today, one that pre-empts any real and meaningful investment in anything—a true postmodern position in which no one has to take responsibility for their actions while all the more emphasising their own background, identity, politics, privilege, or lifestyle.

'As if' also functions as a rhetorical device through which discourses of others—women, queers, BIPOC, the disabled, the neurodivergent, and other minorities—are regularly undermined through gaslighting: as if a particular post was true, White cishetero men of the internet say, while it is just a lie, designed to undermine White men, as they claim. 'As if', then, becomes a kind of twisted phenomenology through which netizens aggressively and forcefully aim to advance their own position or what they believe in. No other perspectives are tolerated. The internet has become a space where fantasies are constructed and exchanged, all of which serve to bolster individual narcissism and group ties. While knowing that in reality the kind of relations, dynamics, and arguments that are staged have an empty core, it is worthy of holding on to them nevertheless. Real change and empathy take effort—they would be, as it were, too long to read.

Those 'as if' sentiments rely on a fundamental *abstraction* of things. Perversion and psychosis both require an opening of floodgates through which new Symbolic articulations may burst forth. Dis/inhibition demands immediacy and frequency. Just as we are reduced into our data through a dis/individualising process in social networks, so too are ideas reduced into their simplest and most abstract form in order to be circulated at a faster pace and a greater volume. The point of texts are in their externality, their capacity for a next, for building a collection. It is here that we see how capitalism has bent our way of consuming texts and images as such, affecting the way we see. Dis/inhibited networks have fundamentally altered our way of reading, our very gaze. If the world of the psychotic seems bizarre in its explosion of nonsensical signifiers, the world of the pervert, it seems, is *cute*.

Chapter 3

The Cute Subject

The Violence of Cuteness

The girl is youthful. Her pink, puffy hair is tied in a twintail, framing a childlike face with large expressive eyes full of sparkles that accentuate her innocent smile. On her little frame hang two abnormally gantuous breasts from which her bikini top has all but slipped, revealing nipples the size of the palm of her hands, both of which she squeezed to excrete a white substance that connects one nipple to the other around her back like a jump rope. Her playful posture suggests that is exactly what she is doing: skipping. Meanwhile, the boy, sporting a no less youthful look and wild, yellow hair that spikes diagonally upwards almost as long as his arm, can be seen squeezing his penis in a proud, heroic posture. It also excretes a white substance, no less magical in its trajectory, onwards and upwards, forming a huge loop above the figure like a lasso. These are not characters from some strange fetishistic porn. They are sculptures by Japanese artist Takashi Murakami, produced in 1997 and 1998 respectively, titled *Hiropon* (roughly 'tired hero') and *My Lonesome Cowboy*. The former was auctioned for close to half a million US dollars at Christie's in 2002 (Christies 2012), while the latter was sold for US \$15.2 million at Sotheby's in 2008 (Douglas 2011).

Takashi Murakami is a spearhead figure of the Superflat movement, a wave of contemporary Japanese art that took the scene in the late 1990s and early 2000s. The movement explores the concept of flatness, both in terms of the visual language of 2D Japanese pop culture often utilised in the artworks as well as the shallowness of consumerism that they believe has come to define their era (Drohojowska-Philp 2001). His contemporaries and successors in the movement, such as Chiho Aoshima and Yoshitomo Nara, often convey a sense of childhood innocence warped by a haunting sense of loss, pain, and loneliness. Aoshima's childlike faces sport characteristic eyes that are dead and hollow in their colours, the figures often entangled with their habitat through hair, vines, or bondage ropes, while 'Nara's large-eyed children are frequently presented as maimed and wounded, or upset and distressed,' writes Sianne Ngai (2005, 820). Superflat also has intersections with the Ero-Guro movement, a shortening of erotic-grotesque, a related movement in manga (Japanese comics) that conveys sexual situations with strange, fetishistic, often violent and repulsive elements. In this way, both Superflat and Ero-Guro can be seen as particular artistic interrogations of *jouissance* apropos of innocence in contemporary society.

Superflat, Ero-Guro, and in fact much of Japanese pop culture can be seen as revolving around the concept of *kawaii*. Sharon Kinsella (1995) and others have claimed that Japanese pop culture has managed to occupy such a strong position, taking the world by storm in the 1980s and 1990s, precisely because of *kawaii*. It has been called 'so much a part of the Japanese spirit' (May 2019, 61), a post-war reaction forming 'monotonous ruins of a nation-state, which arrived on the heels of an American puppet government' (Murakami 2005, 100-101 in ibid, 62). By 1992, *kawaii* was 'the most widely used, widely loved, habitual word in modern living Japanese' (CREA 1992, 58, cited in Kinsella 1995, 220-221). The word is often translated as 'cute', and while it is not wrong, it misses much of its Japanese etymological roots. Kinsella writes,

Kawaii is a derivation of a term whose principle meaning was 'shy' or 'embarrassed' and whose secondary meanings were 'pathetic', 'vulnerable', 'darling', 'lovable' and 'small'. In fact, the modern sense of the word *kawaii* still has some nuances of pitiful, while the term *kawaisou*, derived directly from *kawaii*, means pathetic, poor, and pitiable in a generally negative, if not pleasing, sense. (Kinsella 1995, 221-222, italics ours).

Sharon Kinsella (1995) and Sianne Ngai (2005) have both analysed the link between cuteness and mutilation. The obsession for cuteness is vicious: it is not merely a passive search of childlike helplessness to elicit a feeling of warmth, but an active movement of mutilating the object, enforcing its pitiable position. The relationship of cuteness to the visual and the optic, the desire to see and be seen, is obvious—the eye, a part-object so prevalent in Murakami's works and other spheres of Japanese pop culture—is often elevated into a key signifier of *kawaii*, sparkling and gazing in all of its dramatic glory. But cuteness is also tied to an oral fixation. Murakami's *Mr DOB* character is often portrayed with vicious teeth, and one of his largest murals is that of *Tan Tan Bo Puking* (2002). Ngai takes Nara's food-related objects and the expression 'You're so cute I could *just eat you up*' to exemplify this, highlighting 'the aggressive desire to master and overpower the cute object that the cute object itself appears to elicit' (ibid, 820, emphasis in original).

To understand the visual language of the internet, it is important to take a detour into the concept of cuteness and how it relates to violence and bodily anxieties. Previously, we have taken a look at how these anxieties manifest themselves and become fertile breeding grounds for prejudice, hate speech, conspiracy thinking, and other things that make the internet the 'inverse Hydra with a hundred assholes' that Laurie Penny (2018) describes. Let us now interrogate the origins of cuteness, so prevalent in Japanese culture of the 1990s but also influential to the early internet, and eventually taking the forms of selfie filters, memes, emojis, and chat message stickers we see today.

The Online Militancy of the Cute

The injunction to make all things cute is also apparent in the trend of *moe gijinka*. Literally translated as 'cute anthropomorphism', *moe gijinka* (or simply *gijinka* for short) is a fan-produced movement in various image-oriented Japanese social websites such as Pixiv where artists and fans would create anthropomorphised versions of various abstract concepts from computer operating systems, organisations, to diseases. In the mid-2000s, when the Japanese and Western internet started blending together in certain junctures, *gijinka* started gaining popularity.

Unlike our standard memes today, the remixability of the *gijinka* trend is much more complex than taking an image of certain objects and typing a caption in a certain font with certain linguistic rules. But in its complexity, *gijinka* opens up the space for depictions of cuteness that are much more political in nature. These range from the relatively innocuous Earth-chan, depicted as a girl with a flat chest who expresses annoyance at being called flat, making fun of the Flat Earthers we discussed in Chapter 1. Then there is the more politically active ISIS-chan, a melon-loving girl created to disrupt online ISIS propaganda by hijacking ISIS-related hashtags and flooding social media with messages such as 'knives are for cutting melons' to disrupt the search for terrorist activities and messages. There are those that grew increasingly racist in their evolution, such as Ebola-chan who was created as a tasteless joke and later utilised by racist groups to spread actual anti-African propaganda and hoaxes, supposedly worshipped for the elimination of Africans in regards to the 2013-2016 West Africa Ebola outbreak. And finally there are those created out of ill-intent, such as Winter-chan, with users directly admitting that the creation and dissemination of images of her character is an express wish that a harsh winter will come and kill the Middle Eastern refugees in Europe.

In the comparatively much more benign spectrum of militant online behaviour apropos of cute characters, we have the K-Pop fans. During the 2020 Black Lives Matter protests in response to the tragic death of George Floyd, reactionaries in the form of White Lives Matter and Blue Lives Matter began popping up, as well as calls from police departments to report protest violence in order for them to be able to make more arrests. While the popular idol group BTS managed to raise over US $1 million in less than 2 weeks, its fans (known, amusingly enough, as ARMY) along with many other K-Pop fans on Twitter initiated their own movement to derail the reactionaries and disrupt the police. They did so by utilising fancams—i.e. fan cameras, a term initially used to denote fan recordings of K-Pop concert footage but now also encompassing fan edits of various materials—to take over racist hashtags and flood police servers that ran the iWatch Dallas app (Romano 2020), not unlike the ISIS-chan spam activism mentioned earlier. As a result, anti-protest reporting and racist sentiments became disrupted, iWatch became unusable for some time, and messages failed to achieve any meaningful trends on Twitter.

This militancy is not unheard of. K-Pop fans are known to spam fancams in unrelated discussions and various comment threads, much to the annoyance of other participants. The celebrities are called idols, and many fans are indeed religious in their support, calling themselves 'stans'. This term is now often used synonymously with 'fan', or as its verb form to be a fan of something. However, the word connotes a much more obsessive position. The word has dark roots in Eminem's 2000 song of the same title that tells of a fan named Stan who kills himself and his pregnant girlfriend by driving off a bridge and blames Slim (Eminem's alter ego) for the death. Slim could have prevented the murder and suicide if only he would reply to his letters: 'you coulda rescued me from drownin',' he writes—for us only to find out in the next verse that Slim writes back after all; it was just that the reply did not reach him in time. Although most of Stan Twitter would not develop suicidal and murderous intent upon being ignored by their idols, the structural similarity should not be lost on us: Stan's cries are pleas of recognition by the Other. In Eminem's song, Slim occupies the position of the Other for Stan. On Stan Twitter, the digital space itself— the tweet threads, the metrics, the number of views on fancam videos, etc.—is the Other. Fortunately, this digital Other always replies: we can see our message out there, the view count going up, maybe some likes and retweets.

This fantasmatic nature is, of course, fully understood and strongly reinforced by the capitalist infrastructure upon which idols are produced and managed. The highly exploitative nature of the idol industry, both in Korea and Japan, has been extensively researched (see e.g. Kuwahara 2014): there is nothing pleasant about seeing underage children being put into rigorous training regimes and constant surveillance, with shaming and bullying around every corner, forced to maintain a certain body weight at all times and being forbidden from any sort of romantic relationship throughout the course of their career. While some might argue that the J-Pop industry is relatively softer (or at least tends to hide their exploitation better), both J-Pop and K-Pop romanticise this aspect as a heroic struggle that idols and idol trainees willingly undergo to achieve their dreams, furthering their appeal to the fans.

This militancy of the fans has to do in large part with the fact that idol groups are reproduced with particular structures that elicit care and support, as well as bringing a sense of familiarity to each new group. They have leaders, not in the sense of a lead singer or dancer but a sort of charismatic figure that will lead the group towards their dreams and pull them together in all of their hard work. K-Pop idol groups also highlight the *maknae*, the youngest member of a group, often to bring out the affectionate brotherly bond in their collective struggle. J-Pop idol academies such as the highly successful AKB48 and their sister groups wear characteristic schoolgirl-inspired uniforms, with calls to fans to support them and allow fans to shake their hands upon buying their music at concerts or other events. If J-Pop has *kawaii* and *moe*, K-Pop has *aegyo*, often portrayed as certain feature segments in reality shows and videos where idols conduct certain cute actions like singing nursery rhymes.

These staples of the idol industry can be thought of as a set library of a visual language of cuteness. They recombine into each other by interweaving certain signifiers in the same way that *gijinka* are brought forth, dressed up, and given personalities according to the characteristics of the object they represent or parody. Cat ears, twintails, schoolgirl uniforms, maid outfits, pastel-coloured hair, and hand gestures of peace and love have become signifiers of cuteness through their infantilising nature. But more than that, they have become iconographs in a cultural database.

Take Apart, Categorise, Collect

In his classic study of *otaku* culture, Japanese cultural critic and philosopher Hiroki Azuma (2009) argues that the phenomenon has a long history which is not inherently established in Japan or qua Japanese culture but also through influences from US culture. The *otaku* culture has existed since the 1970s and can be defined, broadly speaking, as people, mostly straight men, who are deeply attached and devote themselves to niche hobbies such as manga, anime, and games. Despite its offensive roots, the word has come to be embraced by fans of Japanese pop culture and is now generally regarded as no more offensive than 'nerd' or 'geek'.

Azuma conceptualises *otaku* culture as a product of the postmodern turn. For him, modernity can be portrayed with a model that is characterised by layers: an outer surface layer of people's consciousness, and a lower 'grand narrative' layer of ideology below. Postmodernity, on the other hand, works like the internet:

> On the Internet, rather, there is a distinct double-layer structure, wherein, on the one hand, there is an accumulation of encoded information, and, on the other hand, there are individual Web pages made in accordance with the users 'reading them up.' The major difference between this double-layer structure and the modern tree model is that, with the double-layer structure, the agency that determines the appearance that emerges on the surface outer layer resides on the surface itself rather than in the deep inner layer; i.e., it belongs on the side of the user who is doing the 'reading up,' rather than with the hidden information itself. In the world of the modern tree model, the surface outer layer is determined by the deep inner layer, but in the world of the postmodern database model, the surface outer layer is not determined by the deep inner layer; the surface reveals different expressions at those numerous moments of 'reading up.' (Azuma 2009, 31-32, emphasis in original)

This layered structure with predefined parts works very much hand-in-hand with the menu-driven form of online identity creation (Nakamura 2002, see also Bucher 2012), applied to a wider context of discourse formation and consumption. In a Lacanian reading, this database model can be understood as the turn from the Discourse of the Master to the Discourse of Capitalism as we have outlined in Chapter 1, with the outer layer being the Subject and the lower layer being the Master. Azuma's postmodern turn, then, is the flip of the two positions, where instances of the capitalist Subject are different expressions of the Market. His inverted notion of the 'reading up' is the downwards arrow of the Discourse of Capitalism, from the Subject to the Market.

For Azuma, the rise of the *otaku* in the 1970s is symptomatic of a desire for grand narratives in a world that had lost such narratives—i.e. a desire for a stronger efficacy of the Symbolic Order. This desire animates much of the cultural discontents today, as we will continue to analyse throughout. In the Japanese context, Azuma reads the *otaku* as born out of a 'trauma of defeat' (ibid, 15) of traditional Japanese culture and masculinity post-World War II, just as incels are similarly born out of a self-proclaimed trauma of a wounded masculinity.

By the 1990s, Japanese *otaku* culture is accustomed to a loss of the grand narrative and functions through a kind of superficial immersion into texts. Azuma theorises this as the database mode of consumption, i.e. consumption via *taking apart* and *collecting*. The database animal—his term for the postmodern capitalist subject—does not merely consume small narratives, but rather takes them apart 'into elements, categorised, and registered into a database' (ibid, 47). They are then brought together again in endless variations to be collected and modified further, such as in the case of *gijinka* and idol industries discussed above. Cat ears, twintails, and pleated chequered skirts, as well as personality traits and behaviours such as the leader and the *maknae*, are all parts of this database. All are signifiers that have been taken apart from their predecessors and registered into a larger cultural database to later be recycled into new characters. The rapid speed of growth of K-Pop and anime thus relies on the export of a fantasmatic structure that can dominate the cultural landscape, after which individual products can directly fit into this structure. In a sense, database animals are subjects that *already enjoy* the very objects they are supposed to enjoy before these objects actually *exist* (as cultural products on their screens or on the stage)—capitalist subjects par excellence.

Azuma, after Hegel, calls this subjectivity 'animalistic' in nature. He goes on to argue that *'the desire for a small narrative* at the level of simulacra and *the desire for a grand nonnarrative* at the level of database is a structure that generally characterises subjectivity in postmodern society' (Azuma 2009, 86, italics in original). Since objects of desire can be easily obtained, he argues that humans have become animals. This is where we disagree with Azuma. In the fantasy sustaining the capitalist subject, of course, the database animal is true. In capitalism, around the corner, all consumer needs can be satisfied with immediacy. Humans can be reduced to animals via the database, via the endless collection of data and the incessant movement of taking apart and collecting. But we argue that things are more complex. The database animal is the capitalist Subject that *denies its unconscious,* sanitised of the Real traumatic core of its bodily existence, reduced into its capitalist Imaginary.

The database, rather than a machine of desire fulfilment, is thus a machine characterised by its constant failure to serve this very purpose. On the level of the simulacra, i.e. the agent, we find an injunction to take apart and collect. It is a mutilating desire, a cute superego. On the level of the database, i.e. the unconscious, we find a desire not for a grand non-narrative but a Knowing Market. For us, the database animal is not the Subject, but rather the ideal ego of capitalism, a subject formation we must aspire to. As such, we must understand 'animal' not in the sense of easy access to objects of desire, but in the sense that animals are *cute.* In today's global capitalism, we must all become cute.

Alter, Post, Repeat: The Conservatism of Memes

While physical mutilation in the name of cuteness is not unheard of—recall, for example, the horrible foot-binding tradition in twelfth- to nineteenth-century China, or how intentional breeding of certain dwarfish traits in pets to make them more cute generates much controversy until today—cuteness mostly relies on behavioural mutilation. Sharon Kinsella writes:

> Being cute meant behaving childlike—which involved an act of self-mutilation, posing with pigeon toes, pulling wide-eyed innocent expressions, dieting, acting stupid, and essentially denying the existence of the wealth of insights, feelings, and humour that maturity brings with it. (Kinsella 1995, 237)

An early form of online behavioural mutilation in the name of cuteness can be seen in *Lolcats*, images that depict cats accompanied by *lolspeak* captions. The linguistic style of *lolspeak* relies on spelling mistakes and grammatical errors. In fact, much of the online spheres of communication tend to integrate spelling mistakes and glitches, such as the term *'pwned'* in video game culture (i.e. 'owned', lost completely) and 'bottom text' in automatically-generated image macros (i.e. generated by not entering a second part to an image caption). On Twitter, it is customary to utilise non-grammatical capitalisation and a lack of punctuation. In AI-generated writing, much of the comedy comes from its mutilated logic, resulting in an often absurdist narrative so characteristic of internet humour. Emojis and chat stickers add a cute dimension to daily conversations via the use of images in service of frivolousness.

In *Understanding Comics*, Scott McCloud (1993) provided a theory of the picture plane, a triangular map of signifiers between photographic reality (visual resemblance), letters (iconic abstraction), and geometric shapes (pure abstraction).

The morph into cuteness, then, can be understood as the shifting of signifiers from photographic resemblance into becoming more letter-like, just like how a smile becomes a colon and a closing parenthesis. Many cute characters lie between the

The Picture Plane

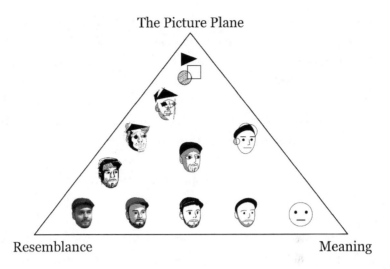

Resemblance   Meaning

Figure 3.1 Authors' reproduction of McCloud's Triangle

photographic and the letter, with their voices (speech bubbles) and excretions (tears, sweat drops) representing additional dimensions of *jouissance*. This is why we can see an awkward-smiling, profusely sweating grizzly bear covered in mud and still think it is whimsical instead of getting creeped out. Once shifted back into photographic realism, however, such a cute image quickly turns uncanny and creepy. Simon May (2019) already theorised the relationship between the cute and the uncanny, but with McCloud we can see how they are precisely the same object being shifted around the plane of signifiers. It is also in this sense that we can understand the logic of the database at work, turning everything into linguistic symbols to be taken apart, collected, and displayed in endless streams of consumptive language.

Lolcats (and internet cats in general) reside in the indeterminacy between cats and netizens. Grammatical errors, glitches, imperfect AI, all reside between legibility and absurdity. Memes are cute, funny, in the sense that they embody what May calls 'the uncertainty principle of cute' (ibid). At its core, cuteness is the indeterminacy of morals and identity. In memes, we can be anyone. Nicholas Cage, Yao Ming, Drake, Obama, Side-eye Chloe, and Bad Luck Brian are no more than the expressions they represent in their image, stripped from their identity, taken apart in the movement of the *otaku*. They are elements in a database, serving more as pictographs than photographs, ready to be reused into infinite varieties to be circulated and collected.

It is in this indeterminacy, this taking apart, this collecting that we find the *objet a*, the cause of desire of cuteness. Memes are the language through which we become cute subjects. In the formulaic nature of memes, the search for the *objet a* becomes mechanical and algorithmic—the fun resides in its very repetition. This expresses itself in the patterned, flowing, and never-ending way that memes circulate.

Memes often embody the 'ironic turn' much of online culture has taken in recent years, where it is never clear what is meant to be funny or serious. They have been hyped and much discussed, particularly in relation to their viral and political nature. While they have been equally celebrated and dismissed because of their radical, subversive, and often tasteless humour, in reality they reveal a conservatism antithetical to the early anarchy of net culture and the self-proclaimed lawlessness of contemporary sites like 4chan and Reddit. Just like idols and *gijinka*, memes work because they take the same *motif* and produce many variations of it, often keeping the same image and changing the accompanying text. This is part of what makes memes funny and easily relatable.

This explosive nature of memes points to a connection between the perversion inherent within capitalism and its psychotic forms as we have discussed in the previous chapter. Memes have a strong connection with trolls: from the earliest practices of 'raids' by 4chan users, the reappropriation of Pepe the Frog in Alt-Right campaigns in the mid- to late-2010s, to the more recent usages of racist *gijinka* mentioned earlier, it is easy to see how internet trolls often speak in memes, even if only to take over or reappropriate existing symbols into new offensive or nonsensical narratives.

To paraphrase Wendy Hui Kyong Chun, memes are *constantly updated so they can remain the same* (Chun 2016). There is an underlying psychodynamic of habit, repetition, and minimal alteration that fits perfectly with the clustering patterns of network culture. While its origin is often unclear, the meme constitutes a remake of the past. As soon as variations of a meme are circulated, they reveal a sense of nostalgia and the desire for it. Like much of contemporary online culture (Dean 2010), they are manifestations of the endlessly circulating Lacanian drive that never reaches its object. Desire knows no end and is always deferred. It is dependent on 'the unavailability of its object' (Ruti 2018, 141) and leaves us wanting 'to keep wanting' (ibid). Memes, too, are based on the principle that they can be reproduced and adapted *ad nauseam*. There is something compulsory about them—if it does not circulate and go viral, it is not a meme. In this circulation we find *jouissance*, ultimately based on the hope for the discovery of the object-cause of desire and therefore infinitely sought and created: maybe your next meme will produce a better laugh, better social connections, and better chances of going viral.

The Endless Collection of the Cute Self

Of course, the desire for the *objet a* finds itself not only in memes but also, and perhaps even more so, in the specular image. This is rather obvious: Who, after all, does not want to look good in front of the mirror? As the culture of the database and the language of the cute start to take hold of society, so too does the compulsion to build images of the cute self.

The ubiquity of camera phones and the ease with which filters can generate cute specular images have made selfie-production an endless pastime, where the perfect selfie lies just around the next snap of the camera, the latest filter, the next social media post. Looking into the specular image is no longer a passive activity but an active one, perpetuated by the logic of the database: larger eyes, smaller nose, brighter skin, cute dog ears and muzzle, cartoon heart stickers, doodles of whiskers, and so on—all linguistic elements of cuteness that can be taken apart and reassembled to build an endless collection of the selfie.

Via Pokémon Go, Žižek (2017) claims that Augmented Reality (AR) technology is the perfect analogy to ideology as such. Ideology is fundamentally what augments reality so that we can see things that are not there. AR, on the other hand, is the technology that visualises our object-causes of desire. This way, we can pretty much derive that cuteness itself is the form that today's ideology takes. The cat ears and whisker stickers of *purikura* (Japanese selfie booths, lit. 'print club'), and afterwards the large eyes, bright skin, and dog muzzle filters of Snapchat and Instagram, are the *objet a* of today's social life. We are immersed in seeking out and constructing cuteness, in others and especially in ourselves, through an injunction to collect signifiers of cuteness.

We must note here that in spite of our critique against selfies, we do not intend to completely dismiss them as no more than vanity. Just like makeup and clothing choices, cute selfie filters, especially ones with smarter settings, can be a safe way for gender-questioning people to explore their performance and identity, for example. The desire to be cute, while always intertwined with ideology, is not a mental illness we must do away with; it is an all too human experience. What we are questioning is the way this desire has been co-opted by capitalism to exacerbate our vanity and insecurities of the self via social media, and how it can mutate into further violence that drives a wedge into ideas of empathy and solidarity.

In later sections, we use the term 'selfie' to refer to the widest, most general sense of one's constructed specular image to be posted on social media. In this very broad definition, one does not even have to physically appear in the image—after all, any collection or stream of digital, online self-representation can be seen as a specular image of the self, regardless of whether such images contain a self-portrait taken from a smartphone. In its most ideological sense, the selfie is an expression built on a cry for recognition.

'Father, Don't You See I'm a Selfie?'

In *The Interpretation of Dreams*, Freud famously discusses the following dream:

> A father had been watching beside his child's sick-bed for days and nights on end. After the child had died, he went into the next room to lie down, but left the door open so that he could see from his bedroom into the room in which his child's body was laid out, with tall candles standing round it. An old man had been engaged to keep watch over it, and sat beside the body murmuring prayers. After a few hours' sleep, the father had a dream that *his child was standing beside his bed, caught him by the arm and whispered to him reproachfully: 'Father, don't you see I'm, burning?'* He woke up, noticed a bright glare of light from the next room, hurried into it and found that the old watchman had dropped off to sleep and that the wrappings and one of the arms of his beloved child's dead body had been burned by a lighted candle that had fallen on them. (Freud 1981, 509, italics in original)

Freud argued that the dream represents wish fulfilment to prolong the father's sleep so that he may dream about his child being alive for a little longer. It is likely that the father senses that something is happening next door and the dream causes him to wake up. Lacan, and later Žižek (1989), have argued that the dream is in fact about the missed opportunity on the part of the father to prevent his son's death and a manifestation of ensuing guilt. What awakens the father is the return of the Real—the father awakens to escape the trauma of his guilt. The Real of the dream is more terrifying than the external reality and the father would rather 'dream on' by being awake to avoid his guilt in the dream.

While this analysis is certainly correct, we suggest another dimension to it: The question 'Father, don't you see I am burning?' is also posed at a much more fundamental level, a level that goes beneath the immediate need to act in the dream situation of rushing to help the son, pouring water over him and saving his life, which implies saving him from falling ill in the first place. The question may suggest that (in the eyes of the father, as he is the dreamer), long before the death of his son, he had already not done enough for him. Perhaps he was not really there for him, did not understand his feelings or concerns, etc. 'Don't you see I am burning?' is essentially a criticism by the son of the father of him not seeing the son at all. The fundamental point as implicitly voiced by the son in the dream is the following: If the father can't even see his son burning, what could he *have* seen in relation to his son before he fell ill? It is thus an expression of a much more fundamental desire for *recognition* and being seen by the Other—an expression voiced by the son, but at the same time an echo of the desire of the father himself. If only the Other had recognised the father, that his mistakes and imperfections are human, and so on, perhaps he would have been a better father, both in his own eyes and in the eye of the Other.

We can underscore this further when we read Freud in the original German as he writes: '*Vater, siehst du denn nicht, daß ich verbrenne?*' The word '*denn*' is significant here: It marks an emphasis of the process of seeing rather than specifically seeing the act of burning itself. James Strachey tried to convey this in the translation through the expression of 'Don't you see…?' but this translation does not put across the severity of the German original. If the father could not even see the flames around the son's body, what could he *ever* have seen in relation to the son? The son's question reinforces guilt in the father, but that guilt is about both not having saved the son and having been a bad or inadequate father long before the son's death (Shengold 1991, 52).[6]

The dream is thus about the desire for an Other who cares for, loves, and validates the Subject in their complete existence. It is a plea to the Other to reassure the Subject of their existence and to fill their lack. This Other is both flawed and weak and yet nonetheless holds the possibility of recognising the Subject — otherwise, if he had completely given up on his father, the son would not have even uttered his question; the Other's lack is acknowledged but the Other (father) is nonetheless regarded as having the ability to validate the Subject's (son) existence.

The word 'see', as uttered by the son in the dream, is crucial in its optics: it relates to the desire for a proper recognition of the specular image. This is how selfies can be read as functioning in a similar manner to the father's dream: they are an unconscious expression of a desire for the Other who validates the subject's existence.

The father believes that his son in the dream Freud discusses felt invisible and unacknowledged, as we have suggested. He failed to see his son, or did not see the full potential in him and the complexity of his being. Secondly, the father feels guilty for not saving his son from his illness, and ultimately his death. Thirdly, it is about the father's own desire to be recognised by the Other.

While other interpretations of the dream may also be possible, we wish to relate it to selfies. The dream functions as a striking metaphor for understanding the role of selfies today.

In taking a selfie, the Subject demands that the Other look at and acknowledge them. The selfie is a form of exhibitionism, but not in the form the term is commonly understood in terms of sexuality, showing my semi-naked or naked body on social media (although such forms of self-representation are also commonplace today). It is a form of exhibitionism in revealing the vulnerability of the subject and exposing a naked hunger for approval and the desire of the Other.

This is how the selfie is fundamentally ideological—cute AR is simply what makes it much more visible as such. Becoming-cute is a cry for a recognition by the Imaginary father. In showing their faces, the Subject communicates that they possess what the Other lacks and desires, and simultaneously exposes their own lack which they hope the Other can fill. They offer themselves up for the consumption and acknowledgement by the Other, but also promise something in return: that they will fulfil the Other's desire. Selfies are thus not just a one-sided act which is about filling the lack of the selfie-taking Subject, but they also signal to the Other that the selfie fulfils the Other's desire; both the selfie-taker and the Other are weak and vulnerable. In return, the selfie-taker expects an acknowledgement of their existence. We can understand this quite literally through responding to a selfie with a comment or a like, in which sense the Other is both imaginary and really existing. The roles of selfie-taker and Other also easily switch when someone comments on another's photos, for example, from whom they have received comments in turn.

Like memes, selfies never cease. Instagram is full of them and many individual accounts show hundreds if not thousands of selfies. The act of taking selfies reveals the demand to be seen—it does not fulfil it. There is always the possibility for more approval, more likes, more attention. As the founder of Snapchat realises, I am no longer everything I have ever done, but I am who I am right now (Spiegel 2015)—the Other requires me to keep posting, to be in constant pictorial communication, so that I know I exist. Selfies, in a broader definition of instantly communicated images of the self, are thus the quintessential feature of the attention economy we have discussed. Like the son in the Freudian dream, it is an undead, zombie-like artefact of our contemporary guilt that haunts and pleases in equal measure.

Our modification of the cry into 'Father, don't you see I'm a selfie?' can then be read as a desperate lament: 'Other, don't you see that my photos are mere dead objects, and the real me is a miserable human being behind the screen with all my suffering?' The original question 'Don't you see I'm burning?' also reveals a distinct disappointment for the son. It is a desperate last attempt at making the father realise the severity of the situation and that he should see his past failures instead of averting his gaze from them. Likewise, the selfie is an expression of hope and hopelessness. The Subject knows that the Other can never fully acknowledge them (as they ultimately do not really exist in the sense that the Subject imagines them); a lack will always remain. The Other can only provide a partial sense of love, care, and visibility. Naturally, the image of myself that I upload to Instagram is not the same and can in no way adequately represent my entire subjectivity and how I (think I) really am beyond the screen. There is tragedy and hope in the selfie, because it embodies an unconscious knowledge of the very inadequacy of its act and the desire it expresses. Yet, the desire still persists. The selfie embodies a reflexivity which reveals and cushions its vulnerability against any potential disappointment. What is worse today than receiving zero likes or comments?

Yeah, Sex is Great But...

As languages of cuteness, selfies, memes, and the visuals of *otaku* culture showcase a similar dynamic. All are symbols of instant, repetitive, and never-ending gratification that functions according to the database logic of established formulas and formulaic practices. Via cuteness, we sustain our fantasy of the Other, but at the same time constantly feel drained by it. We are trapped in platforms, selfies, memes, likes, comments, and shares, and we want to escape. Yet we cannot bring ourselves to acknowledge the unconscious desire to leave all technological relations behind.

Trolls hijack the language of cuteness—memes, but also fake selfies—and the fundamental vulnerability that comes with it, and present this fact right up to our faces: authenticity is powerlessness, empathy is futile. Trolls try to expose the amount of labour it takes to be cute, thereby revealing the sheer gap between fantasy and reality, constantly producing and reproducing the affect of cringe. In their quasi-psychotic decentring of online communications, everyone is always already trying too hard, taking things too seriously—everything is cringe. This is why trolls can be obsessively violent in their actions against trans and neurodivergent people, for example, as in the case of Chris-chan we mentioned in the last chapter, or against SJWs and other people who supposedly care too much. The performance of trolls, their dedication to violence and to eroding cuteness into cringe and contempt, is an ode to the Sadean master of technological relations. Put in another way, trolling presents cuteness in its inverted, true form.

While the Other being called for via the selfie is acknowledged as lacking and incomplete, the ultimate desire that results from the selfie is one for an otherless, perfect Other. Selfies are always addressed at both nobody and actual followers at the same time; to those I know and those that can potentially see it. This double articulation of the selfie embodies the desire for recognition from an Other who is lacking (i.e. actual friends and followers of my Instagram profile whose selfies I can like in return) as well as an otherless Other who is out there in the void of the internet, whose gaze can provide recognition without any actual interaction. This is the ultimate expression of the selfie: a desire for universal recognition without the Other's lack and enjoyment that would intervene. This kind of Other is sanitised and free of otherness, one that can acknowledge the Subject in their complete being that goes beyond the selfie.

As one can derive from the previous chapter, this desire can be perverse or veer into the psychotic. It can be perverse, in the sense that most of us engage with it: We know full well there will never be the perfect selfie—the very nature of dis/inhibited networks themselves means that most relationships will stay shallow, most people will always see me as this collection of images and status updates without ever getting to know my struggles, and so on. And yet, we go on engaging with social media and putting on a mask of authenticity as best as we can, often distancing ourselves through irony and humour. This cry for the Other can also come close to psychosis, in the sense that some of us may believe that such an Other does exist, that some people or a certain group is really able to know every little detail about us. Trolls enforce this belief by making themselves instruments of this evil Imaginary Other, e.g. through doxxing and online harassments. What results is a collapsed world where the Subject is then possessed by paranoiac delusions of conspiracies or other forms of psychotic thinking.

Regardless, there is always somebody else who could see my selfie; my desire is endlessly perpetuated and always deferred. My next selfie, or the next, or the one after might be the perfect one that the Other finally sees. It is the potential that my selfie might be viewed by the Other that brings pleasure and keeps me going, a potentiality that is perhaps better than sex. Perhaps the oft-discussed 'sex recession' of the last couple of years—young people have less sex than previous generations (Kale 2018)— has to do with the status and potential of the image today. 'For the moment, I am not fucking, I am talking to you. Well! I can have exactly the same satisfaction as if I were fucking,' Lacan notes (Zupančič 2017, 1). Both activities are different, yet the satisfactory outcome is the same. Here, we can add to the many variations of the popular Twitter joke: 'Yeah, sex is great, but have you ever taken the perfect selfie that broke the internet?'

Chapter 4

Heteropessimism and Digital Anesthesia

I am an Other

In Daniel Goldhaber's 2018 film *Cam*, the camgirl Alice Ackerman (Madeline Brewer) performs under the name Lola_Lola. In the film, as in real camsites, users are shown paying money which is exchanged for tokens. The more tokens a camgirl receives, the higher up the camsite's public ranking she is listed. Alice wants to be in the top 50 and is willing to perform daring shows in order to get as many tokens as possible. The film's plot progresses as Alice suddenly finds herself locked out of her account and sees someone camming who appears to be her.

The film culminates in Alice creating a new account and confronting the Other Lola live in front of her viewers. She challenges her to play a game of 'monkey see, monkey do' and whoever receives the most tokens wins. A dramatic sequence follows in which Alice repeatedly smashes her head on the table she is sitting at until she bleeds from her nose, presumably to expose the Other Alice as an AI programme, robot, or hologram who is incapable of bleeding. Yet her doppelganger, who has mimicked every move, is also shown with blood on her face. Ultimately, Alice wins the game and Lola sends her the account password. She logs in and deletes 'her' account. The Other Lola has disappeared. The film's last scene shows Alice creating a new profile, using a fake ID, under the nickname EveBot.

The film is about many things. It portrays the common anxieties of our age where others can steal our identity and impersonate us. They do not necessarily have to be real people—even a Deepfake AI can realistically imitate someone's voice and appearance in a video. It speaks to the impossibility of a fresh start online, of leaving our data shadows and traces behind and starting anew. It comments on the excessive amount of time many of us spend on the internet, particularly when our livelihoods depend on online work. Many of us have internalised a similar logic to Alice—in a way, we have all become cammers, broadcasting ourselves to the Other. We are entrepreneurs of our cute subjectivities as we promote our achievements, careers, families, friends, and bodies all so that we may get noticed and fulfil our desires to accumulate likes, connections, dates, matches, friends, and messages—to collect data. Camming and its playful use of nudity, teasing, deception, sexuality, pornography, and, above all, desire is emblematic and was perhaps prophetic of all-too-common forms of representation of bodies today, e.g. on Instagram, Tinder, or Grindr. Bodies are photoshopped, filtered, and often subsumed under a pornographic gaze, all done to increase follower size and make money through promoting brands or themselves, or, in the case of hook-up apps, to 'match' with someone else.

Another aspect evident in the film is the tension between performed authenticity and fantasy. Alice performs a particular persona. Her fans feel close to her, but know that the loving, playful, and intimate attitude Alice puts on is most likely fake. Alice's professionalism is revealed to the film's audience early on when her act of seemingly committing suicide live on cam is revealed as a stunt that she planned with a loyal follower all along in order to drive up her ranking. Alice is the perfect late capitalist subject: malleable, extremely hardworking, with an unstoppable desire to get to the top. 'I'm down to 55. How am I supposed to hold my spot? Not sleep?' she asks another cammer.

Cam is thus a film about the Subject's relationship to an ego-ideal, an Other who takes the Subject's place and acts as them while the actual Subject can only watch in apathy. We get a scenario where reality and fantasy blur, and it is unclear if Alice is imagining things or if what she sees actually happened.

Another copy of Alice emerges, who may be able to perform all the time without ever tiring. Only once we become fully virtual can we get to the top. It is this prospect that frightens Alice. She would like to be constantly on camera so that she can rise to the top of the ranking system, yet once this fantasy is turned into reality, Alice responds with horror and anxiety.

This anxiety is a contemporary one, an anxiety 'not of absence and loss but of overproximity, loss of distance to some obscene and malevolent presence' (Santner 1996, 13). Indeed, for Lacan, anxiety appears when the Subject is confronted with an object in the place of the *objet a*, the object-cause of desire. Something appears in place of the void, something that should not be there. In our context, it is when 'we encounter a complete self confirmed in data, where there should be none' (Gutierrez 2016, 123). Rather than acting in a particular way in front of her cam and seeing herself online, followed by the immediate responses of her fans, Alice sees a copy of herself whom she cannot control. Even though we know that the Market could never make a model of ourselves that will fully replace us, *Cam* shows what might happen once this becomes reality and the kind of anxiety it gives rise to. The online self is thrown back at the protagonist in relation to aspects that go beyond her control. Is not such an anxious presentiment—a persistent worry that *something* might happen to our data and our online selves—an overarching feeling of our culture today?

The Sexual Non-Relation and the Digital

In *What is Sex?* (2017), the Lacanian philosopher Alenka Zupančič writes that sexuality needs to be thought of as ontology. Sexuality is, for Zupančič, not a descriptive name for particular practices, but a concept of a particular contradiction of reality. Sexuality constantly negotiates a form of undecidability. This contradiction of reality forms the very core of sexuality, so it is not a contradiction of established entities or beings, but a contradiction inherent to Being itself. Sexuality is defined by this contradiction, by a non-relation. For Lacan, sexuality is constitutive of and is constituted through the lack. Given his famous argument that there is no sexual relation, Zupančič notes that this non-relation 'is the *inherent (il)logic (a fundamental 'antagonism') of the relationships* that are possible and existing, sexual and otherwise' (2017, 24, italics in original). In that sense, we all struggle with the non-relation of sexuality that binds us into particular relations. An originary sexuality can never exist, as it is always enmeshed within the Symbolic Order. There is a lack of an original signified and the Subject is constituted in the split between reality and the signifier that constitutes it. Sexuality is never about purely bodily enjoyment, because any particular aspect of sexuality, specific practices, body parts, etc., is always already part of particular signifying structures, which allows them to gain pleasure or be pleasurable. It is the 'placeholder of the missing signifier' (ibid, 42).

Sexuality is messy not because of its originary lack, but because of the signifying practices that try to establish a rationale behind it—practices that always fail. In attempting to establish a relation based on a non-relation, sexuality becomes socially repressed. This may happen through practices and discourses such as sexual difference or the oppression of women and queer individuals, for example. It is here at the level of such signifying practices that misogynists, anti-feminists—e.g. incels or Men Going Their Own Way (MGTOWs)—and many other men today fundamentally clash with others. At the other end of the spectrum, one may find a heteropessimistic romanticisation of queer relationships as a more authentic, genuine form of a sexual relationship, thus generating its own forms of antagonisms founded on a denial of the non-relation, as we will discuss later in this chapter. Different and disparate relations are being (attempted to be) used to cover over the non-relation. For Zupančič, such attempts, no matter how progressive or 'democratic' they may be, are always already biased, because they mask or cover over the ontological non-relation of sexuality instead of acknowledging it.

There is something about sexuality that is always unconscious, not because it has been repressed but because it initially appears as repressed. This relates to what Freud called 'primal repression'. It is not that aspects of sexuality are being repressed, contained in the unconscious, but that there is a more twisted relationship between the two and that they are mutually constitutive of each other. Sex always stands in the way of good relations and makes everything difficult. Actual, mutual sexual pleasure is a fantasy, something that is never fully obtainable. Sexuality is inherently contradictory and brings forward the inseparability of the Symbolic Order and *jouissance* in their very heterogeneity. Zupančič develops this in a particularly useful direction for this book when she discusses the relationship between sexuality, the Subject, and the Other. It seems what is so existentially troubling, disturbing, but also arousing about sexuality is its relation to the Other—an actual or imagined Other with their own desires, bodies, unpredictability, moods, affects, and so on. Sex is complicated because there are always implicit and explicit negotiations, expectations, practices, desires, and fantasies up in the air between the self and the Other, and between the individuals involved (negotiating, engaging) in sexuality. Presumably, if only we could 'extract sex from the Other' and 'exempt the Other from sex' (ibid, 28), blissful sexuality, and in turn a blissful life, would follow.

This kind of sexual non-relation extends into online culture whereby the lack is covered over by contrasting and competing relations and signifiers. Online culture is often about the struggle with the Other and how Imaginary relationships and forms of relating articulate themselves through Symbolic means, as in the various examples we have discussed throughout this book. There always seems to be a gap not only between different ideas and people online, but also between their physical bodies and online presence. This gives rise to intense affects and anxieties where the Other always seems to be better able at aligning their online and offline worlds than the Subject ever could. Such online non-relations have a profound impact on our non-relations beyond the online realm.

Incels and the Digital/Sexual Non-Relation

The fundamental non-relation, not only at the heart of sexuality but also at the heart of the way the Subject relates to the digital, leads to a sharpening of alterity and division not only within ourselves but particularly in relation to others we encounter online. Such dynamics can be morbidly illustrated through the so-called manosphere and the incel community in particular (Johanssen 2021). The manosphere is a loose clustering of male online communities (Banet-Weiser 2018) that are all, albeit to varying degrees, anti-feminist and highly misogynystic. There are clear overlaps with the anti-feminism, masculinism, anti-Semitism, and racism of the Alt-Right.

Incels work particularly well to exemplify the underlying logic of dis/individualisation and dis/inhibition on the internet today. Put briefly, incels are young men, mostly but not exclusively White, who have not been in a relationship with a woman for a very long time, if ever. They lament that this is due to their own shortcomings (being ugly, poor, undesirable, depressed, etc.) but more specifically because of the nature of women, whom they dehumanisingly call Stacys, roasties, or femoids. Most women are allegedly superficial beings who are interested in being with 'Chads': White, wealthy, alpha males. Incels are often, as they themselves write, highly inhibited. They, according to their own accounts, suffer from depression, social anxiety, phobia, or social inhibition, particularly when it comes to interacting with the opposite sex.

In a sense, incels are another online community that has

carved out a particular form of identity politics for themselves. It is an identity politics that is fundamentally structured around desire, destruction, and the radical alterity of the Other, othered through the incel ideology. Incels and other members of the manosphere claim that today's men have been undermined by women and feminism. It is women who hold sexual-reproductive power in society, and as a result are free to choose the best, wealthiest, and most handsome men. Incels have taken what they call the 'black pill', realising that everything is hopeless and they will never be with a Stacy. As a result, incels resort to symbolically (and at times physically) attacking and destroying women online and beyond. They dehumanise and disindividualise women through their toxic posts. Yet, incels want nothing more than to finally be desired by and be with a Stacy. Even though they would never admit it, it transpires between the lines they exchange and express.

Their discussions reveal bodies that are torn between desire and destruction, or inhibition and disinhibition. Incels shut down their own love, sexual desire, and fantasy of being with a woman by constantly enforcing hatred and misogyny. They inhibit their own disinhibition and suppress desire and empathy. Incels are obsessed about bodies: Chads' bodies, Stacys' bodies, their own inadequate bodies. They blame the misfortunes in their sexual lives on 'a few millimeters of bone' on their skulls. They share fantasies that show an idealisation and desire of the Chad body which is essentially a fascist body: dominant, muscular, and desired by others. Yet, incels drown themselves in narratives of self-pity and self-castration. They write of mental health issues, inadequate looks, shyness, sexual inexperience, alienation.

While incels, like all of us, live in a superficial world of ideological beauty and the narcissism of the selfie, they respond to such phenomena with what might have been a justified critique of what they term 'lookism'. It is just that their critique is channelled towards the wrong target: cis women, instead of the structure of capitalism in general. It is as if the injunction to keep posting, to get as many retweets, likes, and followers as possible, to post selfie after selfie, to swipe left and right, is attributed to the nature of female desire as such, instead of being designed and incentivised through the architecture of social media and the business models behind them. As a result, incels both affirm and project their own shortcomings onto women in a highly destructive way (see Johanssen 2021 for detailed analyses of such narratives).

While it seems that incels often acknowledge the impossibility of the non-relation rather than try to cover it, this acknowledgement is ultimately perverse: there is a persisting desire for the sexual relation. Incels know that a true relationship is impossible, but they nonetheless define themselves via a lamentation of and defence against this fact. The desire for the Other keeps inserting itself into incels' Imaginary discourse, and they attempt to defend against this by constructing a kind of sexuality without the Other. Alenka Zupančič writes that a kind of conflict-free sexuality is often imagined in this way:

> [I]n order to remove enjoyment from the Other, one has to remove the Other from enjoyment. This suggests in fact that enjoyment and the Other are structured like a matryoshka: enjoyment is "in" the Other, but when we look "in" the enjoyment, there is also the Other "in" it, and so on... Enjoyment is in the Other, and the Other is in enjoyment. This is perhaps the most concise formulation of the structure of the non-relation, the non-relation between the subject and the Other.
>
> If enjoyment is what disturbs this relation, it does so not simply by coming *between* them (and hence holding them apart), but rather by *implicating*, placing them one in the other. (Zupančič 2017, 29, emphasis in original)

Sexuality without the Other is impossible. This is how the manosphere operates and what those men dream of; their discussions are symptomatic of a fantasy of an otherless Other. While incels advocate the annihilation of and independence from the Other (woman), they keep discovering the Other with every such articulation. As a result, they unconsciously construct an otherless Other who can be created and manipulated according to their desires.

While incels present an extreme case, the construction of an otherless Other is not unique to them. Is it not true that our experiences of Otherness—from 2019's 'OK Boomer' meme to men (and women) being haunted by feminine desire—always play with how the Other has a different, better digital/physical relationship from us? Is it not true that social media anxieties often arise from the sense that other people have better alignment between their digital and physical lives? Looking at our user profiles and timelines, there is always a nagging suspicion that we are impostors wrought by pretension, while other people are much more authentic and genuine. And when relationships of other people appear in their failures and inconsistencies, many of us, not so different from incels, tend to point the finger at various facets of heterosexuality.

The Spectre of Heterosexuality

Incels are symptomatic of our current moment of *heteropessimism*, as Indiana Seresin (2019) has written. 'Heteropessimism consists of performative disaffiliations with heterosexuality, usually expressed in the form of regret, embarrassment, or hopelessness about straight experience' (2019, online). The concept responds to a renewed urgency to think about the current status of sexuality. Incels' black pill worldview embodies such a pessimism because they are certain that no woman is ever going to be with them and that everything is hopeless. They are inherently pessimistic about themselves and dismiss any well-meant advice because others can never understand them. Seresin continues, heteropessimism 'generally has a heavy focus on men as the root of the problem' (ibid).

Heteropessimism also often comes with an idealisation of non-straight experience and relationalities. It consists of performative enunciations that are seldom followed by actual consequences. 'Even incels, overflowing with heteropessimism, stress the involuntary nature of their condition' (ibid.) and remain deeply attached to heteronormativity. Drawing on Lee Edelman (2013), Seresin argues that heteropessimism constitutes an 'anesthetic feeling' that works to protect against over-intensity and -stimulation. In that sense, heteropessimism is the perfect illustration of the wider social media conjuncture in which much is said but little is actually done beyond the screen. It talks the talk but never walks the walk. Its 'structure is anticipatory, designed to pre-emptively anesthetise the heart against the pervasive awfulness of heterosexual culture as well as the sharp plunge of quotidian romantic pain' (ibid.) while simultaneously holding onto the very structure of heterosexuality, or covering over the non-relation as Lacan would have it. While expressed and shared online through particular memes or discourses, it works on the individual level and has no sight for real collectivity or social change. 'To be permanently, preemptively disappointed in heterosexuality is to refuse the possibility of changing straight culture for the better' (ibid.)—an inherent enlightened fatalism and defeatism, i.e. what Mark Fisher (2006) called 'reflexive impotence'.

Sadly, incels are not the only group of people who perpetuate a continuous lamenting of the straight experience. One of the implications of heteropessimism, particularly for women, is that queer lives and relationships are imagined as necessarily more fulfilling or somehow better, as Shannon Keating (2019) writes. Additionally, perhaps as a kind of virtue-signalling, people who identify as queer often make remarks such as, 'Are the straight people okay?' or 'Can you imagine being attracted to men?', furthering the hopelessness of the heteropessimistic worldview.[7] On social sites like Tumblr and many corners of Twitter, it is not uncommon to frame abusive behaviours in relationships as something quintessentially heteronormative, conflating patriarchal and other forms of violence with an imagined essential toxicity within heterosexuality and thus obfuscating the possibility of violence in queer relationships. It 'can actually obscure the ways in which gay relationships can also be plagued by toxicity and abuse' (Keating 2019, online).

'Heterosexuality *creates* gendered rules and expectations, rather than the other way around' (ibid, italics in original). But so do many queer sexualties. All of those forms are Symbolic identity politics that are conceived, circulated, debated, and policed within online spaces. They work according to specific images, vocabulary, and symbols that create particular in- and out-groups. From chauvinism to cancel culture, no political spectrum is exempt from an essentialist obsession towards these signifiers. Feminists and anti-feminists are thus united in uncertainty and caution about how to live, have sex, and love together. Yet, they both remain invested in feelings of heteropessimism, because of its inhibiting, numbing, and anaesthetising effects. Moving beyond heterosexuality or embarking on changing it, Seresin argues, means potential disappointment, instability, and uncertainty. Something that is defended against by critiquing while remaining deeply attached to it.

From a Lacanian perspective, heteropessimism can be seen as an acknowledgement of the non-relation which is simultaneously inhibited or negated, covered over with a kind of *sexual realism*—as in the notion of 'capitalist realism' that Mark Fisher (2009) theorised. Straight experience and culture is doomed, but we might as well stick with it for a lack of a better alternative. This sentiment follows the incels' black pill worldview, but is shared more widely by many people today than one might initially think.

While heteropessimism is a general symptom of today's capitalist technoculture, it is differently felt and embodied by various genders. It is also differently experienced by incels, and men who are not destructive or violent. Yet, the underlying structure of this phenomenon is the construction of heterosexuality as a master signifier, a quilting point around which other signifiers form stable relations. Master signifiers 'often appear then as those unarguable aspects of a discursive position, as those self-validating points of attachment to a broader ideological or personal worldview' (Hook & Vanheule 2016, online). In itself, the master signifier does not harbour any real meaning. Instead, it performs an empty gesture of self-referential closure whereby all other meanings and signifiers are stabilised. Yet, this is something that those who cling onto particular symbolic identities, such as heterosexuality, do not (wish to) see. This is how heterosexuality is able to embody different qualities for different subjects within the discourse of heteropessimism. It remains the anchoring signifier to fall back upon within a discourse that is nonetheless critical of it. This is reinforced by the fact that heterosexuality is itself ideological, particularly as it often expresses itself as heteronormativity.

The master signifier not only means an ordering force within a psychosocial universe but also a passionate-affective investment by the Subject in that ordering function (Hook & Vanheule 2016). Yet, having been decentred by queer sexualities, heterosexuality seems to have lost such a function. Queer sexualities challenge the discursive power of covering over the non-relation of sexuality via heterosexuality by proposing different alternatives of sexual relations. This is a good thing: in its history, queer sexualities have never enjoyed a privileged position, and for much of the modern world, have been violently oppressed in the name of protecting a supposed essential sanctity of heterosexuality. We must be clear that what we problematise with heteropessimism is not the fact that it decentres heterosexuality a little too far, but that it *does not go far enough*. In heteropessimism, heterosexuality is still present as a master signifier, though now only as a kind of spectre, a nostalgia that is hated and desired in equal measure.

Such essentialising of heterosexuality is not only ideological, because it covers over the non-relation, but is also met with pessimism, regret, and various fantasies which articulate it differently for different individuals and communities. 'The magic of the master-signifier in the ideological field is that it is able to knit together different constituencies, appealing equally, albeit in very different ways, to a variety of classes who are otherwise opposed in their political agendas' (Hook & Vanheule 2016, online). In the case of incels, there are misogynist fantasies of the Stacy and of creating anime or AI sex slaves, as we discuss below. In the case of cis people, there may be fantasies of more conservative heterosexual relations (if only she was more soft-spoken, if only he was more manly, and so on), or, as Keating (2019) and Seresin (2019) note, fantasies of non-straight relationships and experiences. Either way, heterosexuality remains intact as the desired master signifier. Yet, heteropessimism serves as a kind of social bond that brings disparate and antagonistic subjects together, for which the desire for a master signifier presents different scenarios. After all, 'the more a master-signifier is heaped with imaginary contents and meanings, the more open and vacuous it becomes' (Hook & Vanheule 2016, ibid).

Such dynamics illustrate contradictions between the Symbolic and the Imaginary.

Heteropessimism articulates itself at the Symbolic level where heterosexuality is held onto, and yet, for many straight women, queer sexuality is constructed at the Imaginary level as something better or more fulfilling—a fantasy often reproduced by the queer community itself who portray themselves as better than straight culture, as we have mentioned earlier.[8] But this contradiction is never resolved because everything remains as it is and no change follows for those invested in heteropessimism. Such dynamics are ideological in so far as they isolate heterosexuality itself as a universal category which is agreeable to diverse individuals and groups rather than focusing on particular, contextual dimensions that may be shaping why someone feels disappointment in their romantic life, partner, or in themselves. Rather than being, or arriving at, the master signifier—which functions as a final guarantor of meaning—the establishment of heterosexuality as a master signifier is endlessly deferred and yet desired by heteropessimism.

Meanwhile, those that remain in heterosexuality often feel an injunction to move towards non-monogamy, whether through casual swinging or attempting a fully polyamorous relationship. While there is nothing inherently wrong in polyamory, and there are many positive things in regarding one's sexuality and relationships as a work in progress rather than holding on to any essentialist finality, the idea gets further complicated once new and ultimately impossible fantasies of true sexual relations come into play. Just like other queer sexualities, polyamory is often touted as a better and truer form of love, a love that is ultimately more fulfilling than monogamy. Furthermore, this often leads to instances where monogamy itself is looked down upon as being too conservative, a sign of pathological jealousy, and so on—clear signs that polyamory is often just another manifestation of heteropessimism.

We argue that it is the very contradictions of heteropessimism—the lamenting of the failure of heterosexuality, the occasional envious glances at queer culture, the dreaming up of new sexual relations—all while holding on to the fantasy of heterosexuality—that provide many subjects with *jouissance* today. To operate under the master signifier is to be rewarded with libidinous gratification as it is a response to the non-relation, to the inexistence of the sexual relationship. It is only logical that some wish to reassert heterosexuality as a master signifier when confronted with the Real of sexuality.

Reasserting the Master

While incels embody a contradictory relationship to their own identities and views of Chads and Stacys, they express a wish to 'ascend', as they call it, to assume a new proto-fascist masculinity as we have discussed above. This type of masculinity is exemplary of a desire to return to Lacan's Discourse of the Master and how heterosexuality, albeit coupled with heteropessimism, remains such a discourse for incels. Recall how the Discourse of the Master (see Chapter 1) designates the Master as commanding the master signifier, and all that is produced by the Slave is appropriated by them. This is a totalising discourse in which the Master (Nation, God, etc.) must show itself as an all-knowing and perfect being without weakness.

The misogynist communities, such as incels and MGTOW, embody such fantasies in which they can reign over women, where women exist to serve them and do as they say. Incels' particular form of kingdom—the inceldom—is based on a perverted form of heteronormative recognition grounded in female submission. Incels, as well as the Alt-Right more generally, desire and often post pictures of past forms of masculinity such as the marble busts of Classical Antiquity, images of bodybuilding, and a general constructed nostalgia for a past in which 'traditional' masculinity was still intact—a time that is, of course, the subject of fantasy. We find such fantasies time and time again in incel discourses that not only dream up AI girls but also discuss how women should act and behave, how they should be incels' 'sex slaves' and serve them. Many incels also proclaim that traditional forms of marriage and femininity should be restored, by which they mean that women should stay at home and serve their husbands.

At the same time, incels take pleasure in their Symbolic castration and celebrate it in the black pill worldview. This is a difference to more outrightly fascist subjects on the internet today, such as those of the Alt-Right, who fully assume the desire for the Discourse of the Master. Incels fantasise about becoming the Master while knowing that it can never happen in reality because they are, by self-definition, doomed. They respond to and inhibit their own desire by pessimism, hopelessness, and toxicity. While incels wish to assume the role of the Master, holding power over the master signifier of heterosexuality, they are nonetheless pessimistic about whether this is ever really going to happen.

Of course, not everyone agrees that heterosexuality as such should be reasserted, even on the Right. MGTOWs (Men Going Their Own Way), for example, advocate a lifestyle in which they will no longer need women in their lives. In his campus tours, Alt-Right figure Milo Yiannopoulos claimed that 'gays are genetically destined to be the high-achieving protectors of Western civilization against feminism and Islam' (Nagle 2017, 81). Nonetheless, the spectre of heterosexuality colours these views all the same. MGTOW's self-realisation can only be conducted in the backdrop of women's absence. Milo Yiannopoulos's outrageous claims are nonetheless balanced, as it were, by his being grand marshal for Boston's straight pride parade (Gstalter 2019) and his own claims that his homosexuality brings him 'pain and unhappiness' (Yiannopoulos 2011, online). In Yiannopoulos, we find a deadlock of masculinist monstrosity: homosexuality gets caught up in, or perhaps only justified through, direct misogyny and anti-Islamism. His conviction on male dominance and wisdom led to a questionable stance that 13-year-old boys should be able to consent to sexual advances by adults, ultimately causing a schism within the Alt-Right itself (Lizza 2017).

In all of these cases, the impossible Real of the sexual (non-) relationship remains a traumatic point, to be covered over by an idealised male sexuality. Their masculinity is always measured against women, either through mastery over them or self-mastery without them. The image of woman is always there, ready to be mutilated through dehumanising fantasies of their physical being and social functions or by replacing them with flat cartoons with little to no agency. Heterosexuality remains a master signifier, suspended in its fall, permuting in various ways, and occasionally appearing as its own negative.

As they are heavily influenced by and reliant on images and memes, from porn, manga, gaming, and tech cultures, it is no coincidence that some men of the manosphere discuss destroying women and replacing them with AI systems, sex robots, or anime characters. In those communities, women are not only entirely absent, but they have been substituted in fantasy by 2D characters. Woman becomes abstracted into a universal image akin to a heavily sexualised manga character, the pubertal dream of male cishet geeky teenagers. From such a perspective, it is only logical that women should be replaced by artificial entities which have sprung straight out of a sci-fi scenario. Given how pessimistic they are about the real world, these men retreat into a narcissistic fantasy world where they can create particular relationships in which they are desired by robotic AI-women and -girls.

Projekt Melody: Fake It 'Til You Make It

In July 2019, the self-proclaimed first virtual anime AI camgirl was born. Inspired by elements of Motoko Kusanagi from *Ghost in the Shell* as well as characters from *Hyperdimension Neptunia*, Melody has acquired a large following and is active on PornHub, YouTube, Twitter, as well as the adult cam site Chaturbate. Like many other virtual idols (i.e. so-called 'V-Tubers' such as

Kizuna AI), Melody is controlled by one or more actual people with motion capture suits.

Since her launch in 2019, she has acquired a devoted following, with fans creating hundreds of memes, fanart, fanfiction, even car stickers. Incels make up a section of Melody's fans. They have taken to intensely discussing *Projekt Melody*, as it is officially known. One writes in the incels.co forum:

> [Melody is o]ne of the first steps to male sexual emancipation via technology. Excellent proof that men can and will prefer something obviously fake that treats them well over something real that treats them like shit...Projekt Melody is a sign of things to come and a step in the right direction. (NoCopeNoHope 2020, online)

Another user writes:

> The foid [woman] in the [motion capture] suit can be replaced and nobody would care or notice. She is completely disposable. This is a great step forward in eliminating female sexual dominance. (NoCopeNoHope 2020, online)

Cam depicts the complete synthesis of the actual and virtual subject as horrifying, but for Melody's incel fans, such a scenario is precisely the desired first step towards AI completely replacing women altogether. Melody could eventually be 'live' 24 hours a day and cam to thousands of men individually at the same time. And unlike the Samantha in *Her* which we discussed in Chapter 1, Melody is here to stay as an excessive representation of *enjoyment itself*, which was created by men for men. Melody stands for an indeterminacy that means an attainment of (desire for) an Other who is in a state of becoming. Chances are that Melody will become even better, cuter, more sophisticated, more arousing, and more submissive. She will potentially become both more and less womanly at the same time.

The possibilities for disavowal and excessive emphasis of character traits are endless for those men. AI technology will advance, and so will the virtual camgirl. This means she promises to possess an object-cause of desire, which men can set their eyes on but one that, unlike real women, will evolve and appear even cuter. Given that AI is still fairly limited when it comes to successfully emulating actual humans, this promise is always deferred, and as such precisely keeps the object-cause of desire intact by being just out of reach. In other words, Melody represents the ultimate fantasy for incels and other men: one that is set but will always improve. It is both static and dynamic. Real females cannot receive an update, virtual ones can—so the crude logic goes.

Melody is, above all, *kawaii*. Like other *kawaii* characters, she is built of common *kawaii* signifiers: large eyes, a youthful look, purple hair, stockings, and sci-fi-inspired sexy outfits. She is a purified object for many men because she lacks all human elements; a virtual being who lives in the timeline together with her fans. 'The performance of cuteness, therefore, can be associated with a heightened anxiety concerning the biological processes which cuteness seeks to disavow' (Black 2008, 40-41). Melody's cuteness relies on the sanitisation of her bodily functions—so much so that even the authenticity of her orgasms is a hot topic of discussion for her fans. But of course, Melody's flatness, just as any form of portrayed cuteness for the Other, is a tension that can never be completely disavowed. The Real of human biology always returns.

Monstrous Signifiers: Kago, Joyce

When the Real returns, it returns with a vengeance. Human biology, sexuality, and all the ways they are captured in streams of images return in their traumatic form perhaps best illustrated in the works of Shintaro Kago. As one of the key figures of the *guro* (grotesque manga) movement, Kago portrays the mutilation of cuteness quite literally, as youthful pretty girls become bizarrely cut up into little squares and layers of repetitive body parts (eyes, faces, etc.), often while still smiling. Some are very sadistic in the traditional sexual sense of finding sexual pleasure in cold-blooded evil. Others portray a subjective dissolution in *jouissance,* as characters have heads split open to reveal candies, chocolates, toy train sets, small animals, flowers, cities, pretty girls, and abstract shapes. But it is in his more formalist experimental works that one finds his genius.

The following four short comics of Shintaro Kago can be found in his 2004 anthology *Kasutoru Shiki* (also known as *Kagopedia* in the 2018 Italian edition). In *The Memories of Others* (Chapter 12), characters encounter a disease called 'panelithis', in which characters are followed by previous manga panels around their head. The characters are aware of their being as illustrations on a manga page, but are nonetheless anxious about the loss of privacy that this brings. In *Multiplication* (Chapter 8), the main character itself is a manga panel, sentient of its nature, desperately attempting to replicate and fill in pages to cohere into a story. The catalyst of its reproduction as an image is a sexual failure that happens on the first page, where a woman complains to her partner that she is unable to reach orgasm. In *Blow-Up* (Chapter 10), another sexual failure causes the splitting of images, but in this story the panels continue to split exponentially until they turn into tiny pixels that form the exact image of the sexual failure that happens on the first page. And finally, in *Abstraction* (Chapter 9), upon yet another failure of a sexual relationship—this time a boy dropping a ring in a pond—two characters discover the mechanism that forms the sequential images of the comic book format they inhabit. They explore a strange world where characters and objects are sliced off at the end of the panels to create the sequential images, but nonetheless remain sentient in spite of their mutilation, and adamant in their continued exploration of the bizarre world even if they have to drag their partial bodies into places they are not supposed to belong.[9]

Kago's experimental works portray the kind of anxiety we are faced with in our digital, image-driven world. In his illustrations, the body becomes literally divided as subjects are disindividualised, collapsing in their structure as they are taken apart and the world loses all coherence. It is also easy to see the undertones of superegoic injunction of images as they overtake any form of coherent narrative in his works. In this sense, Kago's works perfectly embody the dark side of the database logic and the anxiety at the core of selfies and memes that we have discussed in the last chapter. But his focus on the human body and sexuality—more precisely, its failures—in relation to the splitting and decoherence of images and the bizarrely violent nature of their reproduction (i.e. as a disease, a sentient creature, an extra-dimensional depth, etc.) brings him much closer to the pathological core that animates the interplay between our online life and the Real of our bodies.

In *Seminar XXIII*, Lacan (2016) analysed the writings of James Joyce, particularly in *Finnegans Wake*. In its unreadability, Joyce 'subjects the letter to littering, turning it into "rubbish", and constructing a *jouissance* that is, in some senses, Joyce's alone' (Noys 2005, 2, quotation marks in original). Lacan's analysis relates Joyce's writing in *Finnegans Wake* (1939) to his experience in *The Portrait of an Artist as a Young Man* (1916), where he recounts being tied to a fence and beaten up by four or five of his friends as a child. 'He observes that the whole business was divested of, like a fruit peel' (Lacan 2016, 128). It is in this experience, in which Joyce expresses a confusion that he feels nothing and has nothing against his bullies, that Lacan situates 'something that asks simply to take its leave, to be divested of like a fruit peel' (ibid, 129). This slipping away like the skin of a fruit, Lacan goes on to argue, is no less than the slipping of the Imaginary. In Joyce, the soundness of the Real-Symbolic-Imaginary ternary is disrupted, as his world decoheres into inconsistency. *Finnegans Wake* is thus his way of organising his *jouissance* by way of the letter itself, 'turning it into "rubbish"'. Through this analysis, Lacan invents the notion of the *sinthome* as a more generalised form of the symptom, one that does not call for interpretation, but merely a topological organisation of *jouissance*.

Can we not see the same logic at work in Shintaro Kago? Even the precise notions of 'peeling' and 'slipping away like the skin of a fruit' can be detected in his characters, as they peel away their skin or as their heads and faces become opened up like fruits, or as the flat two-dimensional surface of the image slips into a bizarre, surreal 3D space in *Abstractions*. In one of the absurdist sequences of *Blow-Up*, a character's penis is literally replaced by a banana in the next panel, which is then peeled off and eaten by a woman. If Joyce subjects the letter to littering, Kago subjects the panel to serve such a function. The panel takes on a life of its own—once quite literally, in *Multiplication*—and takes over the narrative, destroying any traditional notions of character, plot, and representation. If Joyce's *sinthome* is something that pertains largely to himself and his own experiences of a collapse of the Imaginary, Kago's *sinthome* hints at a larger slipping away of bodily coherence in the advent of capitalist image explosion via social media.

There is a larger connection at play here pertaining to our discussion: in the thoughts of Lacan prior to 1975, the disentanglement of the Real-Symbolic-Imaginary triad is simply another name for psychosis. This is quite simple to see, as both Joyce and Kago can be read as being possessed by language, as it were, endlessly flooding the narrative with meaningless signifiers until they explode and turn to rubbish. This connects our discussion of structural psychosis in Chapter 2—caused by the indeterminacy of the phallus in capitalism—with our current discussion of the sinthome—caused by a decentring of sexual and bodily coherence in social media. We can thus see that the two causes are one and the same: phallic indeterminacy is the loss of trust and coherent understanding of our own bodies and sexualities online. But our current understanding of the *sinthome* via Seminar XXIII onwards shows us that this indeterminacy does not necessarily amount to psychosis. Rather than reducing the *sinthome* into another form of structural psychosis, the opposite move allows for more subtle details in our understanding. We have hinted in our previous discussion in Chapter 2 that the psychotic structure we proposed is different from the psychotic of the clinic. This collective quasi-psychosis, for lack of a better term, points to a collective slipping away of the Real-Symbolic-Imaginary triad due to the inefficacy of the Symbolic within capitalism, as we shall discuss further in the following chapter. But this is not to be understood as a clinical psychopathology into which we are all doomed. Rather, the idea of the *sinthome* allows us to see this as a *topology*. Internet trolls, while banal and violent, are one manifestation of this topology—but they do not have to be the only one.

Today's topology is one in which images have become parasitic in their incessant stream. Faced with the inevitable failure of a sexual relationship, images exponentially multiply and take over our lives in a desperate attempt to cover over (or make up for) this traumatic lack and build a coherent narrative. Our bodies are brought online to be dissected, taken apart, collected to form a Knowing Market that possesses the truth of our desires. Yet, just as in Kago's works, the realities of sexual coercion, defecation, mutilation, and other traumatic experiences continue to disrupt any form of coherence. Nonsensical articulations explode into the scene as the Real returns with a vengeance: our bodies, in the end, are always unreliable.

The Unreliable Body

We live in an age where everything is reliable. The platforms, social media, and apps we use are always on, connected, ready — the moment they crash or lose their connectivity becomes more and more a source of great frustration. In our day-to-day lives, we have to be reliable too, both in private and public, at home and at work. We have to be reliable on social media — say the right things, signal the right virtues — or we risk being cancelled. Unreliability is punished and disciplined, while reliability is rewarded. The constant stress we face leads to mass burnout and depression, and finding its cure — meditation, hypnosis, self-help seminars, to certain kinds of clinical practices — has become a burgeoning industry that promises a reliable stream of economic productivity.

And yet, as Lacan has noted, sexuality is inherently unreliable, giving rise to various means to cover over its failure. We have discussed exemplary cases in this chapter that attempt to do just that: incels, heteropessimism, AI girls, etc. are all particular ways that respond to the unreliability of sexuality and its current articulations in different ways. All express a desire for a totalising master signifier that anchors sexuality in the fantasy of an ideal, authentic relation. Today, it is technology that promises an end to unreliability, uncertainty, and the unknown — an end of the Real. Yet, such desires of reliability remain fantasies. Networked AI is the Username-of-the-Father, but it is characterised by a downwards arrow of consumption instead of a forward enunciation. Its only function is to remind ourselves to believe in capitalism in spite of our full awareness of its inherent unreliability. In the end, there is nothing whatsoever that can ground us, and we are left with an oscillation between paranoia of all sorts (fascist, misogynist, conspiracist, etc.) and an incessant habit of scrolling and posting on social media.

Psychoanalysis teaches us that we cannot rely on our own

memory, consciousness, and rationality. We are shaped by unconscious and affective processes that undermine the very idea of human reliability. The political implications of the different scenarios and examples we have discussed in this chapter are that they operate with a violence that negates or seeks to erase any form of unreliability and contradictory agencies. *Cam* shows what happens once we trade our bodies for an automated, reliable Other; the human Subject can be discarded and has given way to a virtual self. Shintaro Kago's works illustrate that this Other is, in fact, not reliable at all, as its gaze becomes a machine of relentless self-reproduction, image begets image in the infinite loop of capitalist consumption.

But the psychosis of images can be gathered and subsumed by those who wield the means to do so. In and of itself, the internet does not shape the knot of the *sinthome*—the specific organisation of *jouissance*. It is rather the practices of people with the necessary technological means that play precisely such a role. Amid the chaos, power structures prevail. One must always keep in mind that capitalism, while often seeming like an immutable law of the universe, functions by design. Its very architecture concentrates wealth—as well as knowledge production in its most universal sense—in the hands of the few, away from the hands of the many. We all simply play along.

Chapter 5

Playful Perversions: Narcissism and the Gamification of Control

Joe Goldberg, or, Cambridge Analytica Personified

In the 2018 Lifetime/Netflix series *You* (adapted from the 2014 novel of the same title by Caroline Kepnes), we follow Joe Goldberg (Penn Badgley), a bookstore clerk who stalks his way into becoming the ultimate prince charming of his love interests, the first season's being Guinevere Beck (Elizabeth Lail). The series presents a chilling atmosphere as we see Joe's increasingly violent actions, made all the more uncanny by his narrations on how he is committing all his egregious crimes to protect her. Joe claims to do this out of love, although we, the viewers, know that what appears to be love (especially to Joe himself) is none other than an obsession towards a totalising knowledge of the Other, to become a master of Beck's life by realising all of her desires, which, of course, he claims to know best. In fact, the series goes as far as to show that all of Joe's traumatic reactions come from realising a gap in this knowledge, from discerning there are things he had missed.

While Joe is no more tech-savvy than the average person, his violence is visceral: stealing other people's phones, reading all of their messages, going through their laptops, impersonating their social circles, and outright lying and manipulating others in their faces. The creepiness comes precisely due to the fact that almost anyone can do what he does to gather information; if we are willing to forgo all sense of integrity and violate other people's privacy, a look into social media and a browse through private conversations can give you most of the information you need about a person and their social circle, as well as their aspirations and fears.

The series falls short of being a critique of the information society and instead goes on to localise the problem in Joe's own mental health issues and past traumas. However, as we have discussed in the first chapter, it is easy to see that Joe's desire is the same one that lies beneath capital today, as he claims to mine Beck's data for her own personal comfort (i.e. making sure she socialises with the right people). As Joe states in the tenth episode of the second season, 'It isn't hard to convince somebody you love them if you know what they want to hear.'

Those same words may as well have been uttered by a figure like Alexander Nix, then-CEO of the now-infamous Cambridge Analytica. In fact, are Joe Goldberg and Cambridge Analytica not two embodiments of the same obsession? If Joe commits his violations of privacy to take charge of his twisted romantic life, Cambridge Analytica does so to influence 'over 100 election results in 32 countries', according to whistle-blower Christopher Wylie in *The Great Hack* (dir. Noujaim & Amer 2019). It is easy to be repulsed by Joe's actions, but he holds no candle to Nix's claim of 'close to four or five thousand data points for every individual...in the United States' (ibid). This becomes increasingly creepy when we consider that the data collected by data mining companies begin before individuals have the right to vote—by the time they do, they will have been profiled through thousands of data points.

Repulsive as it is, even years after the Cambridge Analytica scandal, most of us still willingly hand our data to Facebook and other tech companies. And Joe is right: we want to believe technology loves us back, even if only out of dependency on these social tools and the comfort of staying in the social loop. But if mining one's data can be legitimised through narratives of dependency, affection, and comfort, the opposite is also true: there is hardly a clearer declaration of antagonism today than airing one's private data out into the open, or coercing others to consume data against their will, pulling on certain psychological triggers.

Whether we are dealing with stalker issues, political disinformation, or vengeful hackers, one thing is clear: data collection has cemented itself as the primary drive of today's capitalism. *The Economist* proclaimed data as 'the new oil' (2017, online). As such, its production and dissemination become tools of discipline.

Psychopolitics and its Discontents

In the first chapter, we used the term 'epistemology' (somewhat loosely) to mean the entire field of knowledge and its production. The reader might have noticed that we are not using the term to conduct a new epistemological project, such as to sort out what is knowable and not knowable, to propose new methods to justify statements apropos of their truth values, or to speak of things which exist beyond knowledge. However, we are speaking of how knowledge is produced, how and why we partake in such a production, and what power structures are legitimised in this production. In this sense, our project is closer to Michel Foucault's.

For Foucault, knowledge and power are inseparable, not only in the naive sense that those with better knowledge wield more power (tech giants wield power over us because they have all of our data, etc.), but also in the sense that knowledge implies its production through power relations. Of course, this is also Lacan's position as we have described earlier in the book: knowledge production always has a Master in its unconscious, purporting to speak from a neutral place while serving the status quo of established power relations. Here, power should not be understood as a sovereign object which one possesses, but as relational—every interaction of actors, human and non-human, produces power. If Foucault had been alive today, perhaps he would have taken an interest in analysing doxxing, cancelling, and other social media phenomena. After all, these are clear cases of interaction where power is explicitly exercised to control and punish those that more powerful actors have deemed to be morally inferior. Revenge porn, by its very naming, shows exactly this tendency. The more interesting question for us in this chapter, however, is the shift in the locus of power.

Foucault's genius—and one of the reasons that many Marxists (see Bidet 2016; Negri 2017 for recent discussions) steer away from him—was his move to show that power was not a sovereign entity exercised by the oppressors to the oppressed, but rather immanent in all kinds of subject relations. We actively reproduce power in all directions in our everyday actions, habits, communication patterns, choice of fashion, sexual behaviour, and so on. The locus of power, therefore, should not be seen in the context of who owns power, as if power is a discrete top-down entity, but rather what objects and practices must be controlled for power operations proper. Let us illustrate this by following Foucault's arguments. For Foucault, the shift from corporal punishment to the prison system is not necessarily an indication of a more enlightened society, but an effect of the shift of the locus of power. Torture and public executions were commonplace in monarchy, because an attack against the state is an attack against the sovereign body of the king; therefore it is the body that must be punished (Foucault 1977). During the eighteenth century, people began to see crime as a breach of the social contract, hence disciplinary prisons and mass incarcerations became more popular. Power was once about seizing life, suppressing life, ending life. Afterwards, it became a tool that invests in life, controls life as a means of production (Foucault 1978). After the body, the locus of power becomes the management of one's space and time. Corporal punishment and spectacular deaths give way to disciplinary institutions such as prisons, schools, factories, and so on. The gallows and guillotines are replaced by iron bars, factory floors, and school walls.

Because the subject already actively reproduces power, a natural next step follows: internalised self-control. Deleuze (1992) calls this next step the shift from the disciplinary society to the society of control: the enclosed factory floor gives way to an omnipresent corporate spirit, fully internalised as the private ethics of life. However, as Byung-Chul Han (2017) has noted, Foucault hit an impasse when he failed to go beyond the body into the psyche—not the least bit surprising, as he was critical of psychoanalysis and the kind of knowledge of the psyche it claims to produce. Inhibited by his own limitation, Foucault advocates an individualist ethics, a care of the self that is free from biopolitical disciplinary practices, as the praxis of resistance and freedom. However, this is precisely what global capitalism wants you to do: relentlessly enjoy the seemingly endless options it provides, for it is this very freedom that is today being exploited.

My Avatar is Not My Soul

In the first chapter, we have shown the falsity of capitalism's claim to a totalising knowledge: instead, capitalism works on a fundamental *misrecognition* of our desires. Big Data misrecognises our desires by reduction, repression, exclusion, and mutilation in order to fit them into tiny little boxes of the database. Consequently, it has turned us into database animals (Azuma 2009). Throughout previous chapters, we have shown in depth that this attempt at fully domesticating our desires is bound to fail. Its failures can be seen as they etch themselves into our minds and inscribe themselves in our bodies, as the rise of incels and other extreme views on bodies, sexualities, and gender positions have shown. Han's focus on fatigue (burnout, depression, exhaustion, etc.) and what he calls positive violence (over-achieving, oversharing, hyper-attention, hyperactivity) is undeniably illuminating to our understanding of contemporary culture. However, it seems that Han may have overlooked a crucial aspect: perversion, manifesting itself in the various forms of fetishisation of body-images and identity signifiers, exploding in imageboards and making their way into mainstream movements of fascism, racism, and misogyny. It turns out, as Big Data attempts to dismantle the Real, as much as it has claimed to have done so, the Real will always return with a vengeance.

In the same vein, we maintain that the Real of class antagonism can never be fully reduced into internal struggles of the individual. After all, is not self-exploiting entrepreneurship a predominantly middle-class phenomenon? From young mothers reselling children's books and knock-off fashion items on Instagram to tech-savvy urban 20-somethings pitching their latest app idea to Venture Capitalists, entrepreneurship takes on many forms to varying degrees. Certainly, Jack Ma and Jeff Bezos do not exploit themselves in the same way that a 19-year-old single mother of two exploits herself by utilising gig economy applications of freelance house-cleaning services so she could have the so-called flexible work hours. Even at the epicentre of technology companies, entrepreneurship is not a flat phenomenon to which all struggles can be reduced. For all its romanticisation of hard work, the success of entrepreneurship relies on the fact that vast numbers of people will always exploit themselves in a much more vicious manner (e.g. in the cheap overseas labour economy) than the ones at the top. Thus, while Han's insight into entrepreneurship and positive violence has been illuminating, it is not the end-all and be-all of today's form of exploitation. The Real always returns, and class struggle always persists. Capitalism remains, whether through neoliberalism or otherwise, and the discourse formation that Lacan formulated in 1971 holds true until today.

Resistance through seeking an outside of networks through a pre-linguistic subjective position—like what Han (2017) himself seems to be inclined towards—is thus misguided. Language always already contains *its own externality*. Networks *exclude* as much as they include. Big Data, through their very reductionist approach of turning our identities and desires into discrete data points, generate an *excess* that can never be integrated. The Subject can never be properly controlled through psychopolitics or otherwise, since by its very definition, the Subject is that which objects to subjection proper, the kernel that escapes Symbolic subjugation within a discourse. But if the truth of our desires is fundamentally unknowable and will remain so in spite of any means of psychopolitical technology, then the question remains: What, then, is the locus of power in today's psychopolitical control?

Power can seize life, suppress it, and end it through instruments of murder, war, and torture. Power can also discipline life through institutions, turning life into machines to produce commodities. Today, power can gather, reveal, disclose, construct information on, and influence future trajectories of life through digital technology. This turns life into a limitless source of data to produce smart commodities through imbuing ordinary objects with a more comprehensive, personalised profile of one's desires, nudging individuals into certain behaviours. It is true that our psychopolitical era takes the psyche of the individual as the site of control. However, we argue that this must be understood in the proper psychoanalytic sense: the psyche does not contain an inherent subjective truth, but is rather a continuously shifting constellation of signifiers. The Subject is an illusion of the failure of 'I', the Symbolic signifier of myself that can never fully represent myself—and, as such, it is not the locus of power in psychopolitics. That, instead, would be the specular image.

The Monitor Phase and Black Box Controller
In Lacanian psychoanalysis, a child's self-identification begins with a mirror phase, i.e. a moment when an infant recognises

that they constitute an extended body as seen through a mirror, and that others outside of their body perceive them as an object in this manner as well. Although the empirical presence of a mirror and its function for this precise stage of psychological development is not to be taken literally, the concept remains: a human child learns to imagine themself as an object for others and identifies themself with the extensions and limitations of this body they inhabit. Yet this process of recognition always entails one of *misrecognition* as well. The young child may think they are able to accomplish tasks (e.g. walking for long periods of time) which are in reality impossible to master, or can only be accomplished in a clumsy manner at this age. The mirror image stands in contrast to the Subject as such, taking the place of the Subject's self and refuses alienation and fragmentation.

The same can be theorised of what we may call the monitor phase, or the moment when a human child (mis)recognises the data on their screen as an adequate representation of themself in the digital world. From playable video game characters to social media profiles, from status updates to shared memes, active participation in the digital brings forth a rich world of the Imaginary order. This is when the child learns to construct their online identity in menu-forms (Nakamura 2002), entering the world via the dis/individualising dynamics we discussed in Chapter 2. If the mirror phase is the moment in which a child recognises themself in the mirror, the monitor phase is the moment when the child learns to take selfies.

As both the mirror phase and the monitor phase constitute the Imaginary, the two concepts should in no way be thought of as discrete, separate phases. The mirror phase continues throughout life (observing, identifying, and modifying our physical bodies is an activity that never ceases), and the monitor phase is but its extension. However, there is a crucial difference between the two. The specular image produced by the monitor phase can be numerically represented, and is modular, automated, variable, and transcoded—the five key characteristics of new media as presented by Lev Manovich (2001). The specular image is now a mathematical object, programmed and programmable. It is an object of the database, to be taken apart and put back together again in multiple arrangements, each part modified through script, generating an endless repetition of selfies (Chapter 3) that become nodes for Big Data.

Byung-Chul Han was right when he mentioned that the contemporary age is marked by the turning of subjects into projects. With so much plasticity over my specular image and the amount of control that I am told I have over my identity, would it not be best to ignore my fundamental subjective lack and instead focus to live a lifelong project of endlessly constructing and reconstructing my image? I am no longer bound to a representation by my flesh and blood body, portrayed by the reflections of light coming off a mirror which I use to see myself every morning. Online, I can represent myself through a profile picture that has gone through visual filters, AR applications, fancy stickers, and a call-back to my video game avatar. I can truly and endlessly strive to become a cute subject. But these pixels on a screen are not simply a shift in medium with blinking lights and fancy features added on top. As electronic signals, they are also signifiers for the screen, the browser, the app, the server, the server's providers, the targeting algorithms, the advertising companies, the processors on my smartphone, and so on, layers upon layers of codes that network with and act upon one another. As N. Katherine Hayles (1999, 2008) noted, the signifier is flickering. What used to be a system of dots on paper has transformed into electronic signals that are vastly more complex, dizzying chains of signifier-signified relations that shoot off in multiple directions all at once.

It is in these new depths of a flickering signifying chain that we find the operators of power at work today. The flickering signifier is never innocent—in their interactions with one another, they not only signify my past but also attempt to determine my future. More often than not, I am not aware of what signifiers are used to represent me to the tracking applications and advertising companies so they can better track me as a potential customer of their products and worldviews and influence my behaviour in certain ways. More often than not, I am not aware of what signifiers I am actually inscribing online when I utilise certain applications to communicate with my peers. My social life wholly depends on partaking in social activities whose breadth of information gathered about me and the variety of digital footprints that I leave will always be mostly unknown to me. The fundamental question of psychopolitics is thus a question of *writing the self*: What is being written about me without my knowledge? What am I inadvertently writing for others to read?

The mirror phase accounts for the physical body as a sovereign entity of production. Accordingly, its tool of discipline is predominantly *optical*: Bentham's panopticon, Orwellian surveillance state, and so on. The monitor phase provides a new dimensionality to life itself, the depths of machines and signifying chains, layers and networks of codes and information. Its tool of discipline is predominantly *playful*: gamified social reward systems that concentrate power in the hands of those who can pay for it. Your everyday gadgets are black boxes that hide millions of surveillance and tracking devices for your life beneath an almost impenetrable complexity of multiple layers of code and the complex machinery of power behind the writing of those codes.

Hope and Despair

If power can suppress life and discipline it, it can also control it through its very decision on how to make life worth living. Social media and other platforms of the internet illustrate the playful nature of most online cultures today where bright colours, large fonts, short text, memes, clips, and emojis dominate. Interfaces are loaded with metrics, stats, likes, hearts, and numbers akin to the high scores in the arcade video games that many of us grew up with.[10] Reality itself has become gamified. Through playful social media interactions, we perpetuate our own exploitation for data creation. Power has shifted to become participatory, providing rewards and nudges that hook us with enjoyment while keeping us powerless to change the hard-coded rules of the game. The immanent life of childhood has been replaced by the ennui of an endless, obsessive repetition of likes, swipes, and scrolls defined by rigid rules that serve to accumulate data and wealth for the few.

But power is not only active and participatory; it is, above all, *perverse*. As we have previously mentioned, for Lacan (2002), perversion is characterised by a disavowal of Symbolic castration that simultaneously acknowledges it. A perverse relationship is one in which one or more participants desire their own exploitation, humiliation, and disindividualisation. The pervert forces the other into the position of a lacking subject while seemingly treating them with care, love, and respect. The other is lured and seduced into such a relation, but also often actively strengthens it. The destructive dimensions within a perverse relationship are then either disavowed by both the pervert and the one who is exploited (through outright denial, irony, celebration as something positive, etc.) or otherwise silenced through manipulation and coercion.

Heiko Feldner and Fabio Vighi (2018) have argued that we currently live in a time in which capitalism is unable to 'disguise its own growing unproductivity' (ibid, 109). The 2008 global financial crisis exposed the volatility of housing and financial markets and resulted in crushing austerity in many parts of the Western world. Ever since then, neoliberal capitalism has become unable to sufficiently mask its own drive and, crucially, has failed to provide any new narratives through which to ideologically fix and interpellate subjects. The United States and many other parts of the world witnessed first-hand how the system is inherently flawed. The banks are bailed out, yet houses are foreclosed. People took to the streets in various Occupy movements, and a couple of years later the Arab Spring began.

Believing in capitalism seems naive. Much more than the celebrated entrepreneurism of the 1990s and early 2000s, the individual ethos of the world after the 2010s seems to be defined by social media anger at the impotence of neoliberalism. Yet self-help and entrepreneurship is as popular as ever, and many people still have an optimistic outlook that technology will continue to improve our quality of life and solve most of our problems. How is it possible that naive hope and utter despair coexist within the same society at the same time? For Feldner and Vighi, the only answer to such an impotence is the perverse logic of disavowal. They write that the, 'secret objective of perversion, as theorised by Lacan, is not to transgress the law, but to bring back its authority, to the extent that it must appear explicit, inflexible and indestructible — as in the exemplary case of the masochist who stipulates a contract with the strict and uncompromising dominatrix who tortures him' (ibid, 110). This is surely desired by the players of neoliberal capitalism, but also by the majority of the population who are exploited in capitalism because it promises Symbolic efficiency, coherence, and stability.

As the reader may have noticed, we argue that things are slightly more complicated. The instability of capitalism itself, we claim, produces a response that is more complex and more subtle than disavowal. Rather, through its breaking of the epistemological circle (Chapter 1), capitalism amounts to a phallic indeterminacy that always hints that maybe castration never happened (Chapter 2). It is not only that the Symbolic of capitalism is lacking efficiency, but also that the consistency of the Real-Symbolic-Imaginary triad itself is always teetering on the brink of collapse. We are, quite literally, on the verge of madness.

Paranoia and perversion dance in harmony. On the one hand, everything is deadly serious. Incels, truthers, White supremacists, pandemic deniers, and so on function under the belief that various groups possess incredible power (the Jews, the Deep State, feminists and the 'postmodern neo-Marxists', etc.). They reject traditional neoliberal meritocracy and unmask this crisis of capitalism (Bratich & Banet-Weiser 2019). On the other, everything is a joke, and we should keep laughing at our own impending extinction. Amid the interplay of the two, the flower of Narcissus weaves its roots into every facet of digital society.

Narcissus and Alexa

In a myth from Ovid's *Metamorphoses*, the beautiful young man Narcissus encounters his reflection when drinking from a spring, and promptly falls in love with it, causing him to reject all advances by the mountain nymph Echo. For her part, the once-talkative Echo was cursed to only be able to repeat what others have said, never to start her own sentence. When she encounters Narcissus, Echo desperately tries to answer his questions with his own words, an undertaking that was bound to fail. In the end, the vain Narcissus chooses to stay by the spring and turns into a flower, forever looking at his own reflection, while the dejected Echo hides in the mountains and the cliffs, forever repeating the words spoken to her.

Narcissus is a subject that postulates the object-cause of desire in his specular image. This is where most popular readings of narcissism are mistaken: the narcissistic subject is not in love with themselves, but rather with the idealised image of themselves. The narcissist finds obsessive enjoyment in the act of looking into the spring, of *producing* the specular image. A liking of one's own specular image is not inherently destructive—after all, one needs to have a minimum degree of appreciation in one's looks and individual narratives to be a psychologically healthy individual. The key here is not to let one's image become the object of desire as such, to fall into the illusion that our image needs to be perfect for a minimum functioning of our lives. The obsessive, circular motion of producing hundreds of selfies a day, while perhaps annoying to some, is not necessarily pathological unless one grounds their entire subjectivity into the act of selfie-production.

However, the design of today's digital life proves to be a constant challenge to resisting the narcissistic allure. Our social media profiles, the keywords and sentiments of our tweets, our communication records, browsing histories, the cookies tracking us on every website, every part of our data shadow and other information are aggregated into a digital representation of ourselves that capitalism postulates as our true selves. It is clear that capitalism wants us to be a subject reducible to its specular image—in this formal sense, it is not difficult to see the parallel with the narcissistic subject. Narcissus turns into a flower by the spring, a being of pure self-referential desire, so his physical reality can finally reflect his specular image. Do we not find the same echo of this desire in the transhumanist fantasy of reducing humanity into pure data living in the clouds? Metaphors of Prometheus are often the one invoked in these fantasies due to its technological nature, but the reductionist approach to the subject is fundamentally a narcissistic one.

This is how we should read narcissism in relation to the digital space today—not in the crude sense of how culture is nothing more than a stream of endless self-absorption, but in the sense that the functioning of capitalism relies on a constant *reduction* of our lives into a self-lovable, likeable, retweetable, followable collection of images. In return, they provide narcissistic pleasure by providing us with real results and measurable metrics of how much the Other acknowledges ourselves as objects of desire, as we have mentioned in the previous chapter. Dating apps like Tinder provide the perfect example of this, as we voluntarily reduce ourselves into a few images and a bio to get swiped right by another set of images and bio that we have also swiped right. In other words, we desire our own dis/individualisation via platforms. We willingly enter into contractual relations with platforms which perfectly resemble the dominatrix-masochist relationship that Feldner and Vighi write about. In this sense, narcissism can provide a framework of perversion. The narcissistic injunction of global capitalism certainly does.

When there is a Narcissus in love, there is an Echo cast away. Where Narcissus turns into a flower, Echo turns into a repetitive voice—the Real materiality of the signifier, completely devoid of meaning, a nightmarish part-object that obsessively trails after the signifier. The cost of reducing oneself into the self-referential specular image is the production of a remainder that incessantly follows and listens. Isn't it perfect that Amazon's Alexa is housed in a device called Echo? Parallel to the endless stream of data and images we enthusiastically provide our platforms; there is always a remainder in the form of the act of surveillance itself. We are at once coddled through Narcissus and dehumanised through Echo. The anxiety of having our gadgets listening to our every conversation is not lost on us, as exemplified by a joke on Twitter that went viral in 2019: 'My wife asked me why I was speaking so softly at home. I told her I was afraid Mark Zuckerberg was listening! She laughed. I laughed. Alexa laughed. Siri laughed' (Rogers 2019).

Masochists of the Market

The declining Symbolic efficiency of capitalism, then, has been replaced with an Other who should recognise the subject who offers themself up to them via consensual surveillance. In that sense, the absolute dominance of the image and visual forms of communication as we have examined in Chapter 3 is not surprising, for it is inherently perverse. The Subject uses their own 'libido precisely as a cork, a filler or stopgap, aiming to close the chasm in the weakened Other' (Feldner & Vighi 2018, 111).

Here we can read the desire to manifest a physical Other in place of the weakening Symbolic Order as the very desire to imbue the Market with a totality of Knowledge, to serve a Knowing Market. Our selfies, our tweets, our endless participation in the constant flux of exhibitionism in social media is fundamentally an expression to strengthen the weakening Other by making ourselves the instrument of the Other's *jouissance*. This is how we should read Feldner and Vighi's assertion that our libido functions as a cork: by becoming an instrument of the Other's desire, we position ourselves as possessing the very thing that the Other lacks. The object-cause of desire is turned inwards, into ourselves, turning us into a masochist, a pervert subject par excellence. Is it any wonder that we desire our own exploitation? It is through this very exploitation that our narcissism functions; it is an exploitation that serves as the very basis of our love with the specular image.

Our worldview as that of the pervert's should be understood also in a formal sense: the pervert pretends to know what their sexual partner desires, convincing or sometimes coercing the partner that they desire certain practices and objects, thereby displacing the moment of castration to the partner while simultaneously disavowing it. In response to the doubt of the Hysteric, the pervert responds, 'I am not doubting, *you* are doubting, but now you will cease doubting because, through me as your object of desire, you will affirm your unbridled enjoyment!' With this insight, the world's failing belief in capitalism can be seen in a new light. We are not doubting capitalism, we are merely witnessing it doubt itself. This is what makes it possible for us to romanticise self-help and start-up ventures, and maintain a firm belief that technological innovation under today's capitalist conditions can nonetheless improve the quality of life for the world. We only need to fix the cracks within capitalism by utilising our libido as a stopgap, providing the Market with our data so it never stops reaching its *jouissance*.

Byung-Chul Han (2015; 2017) theorises that today's class struggle has become internalised, taking the form of burnouts. We argue that burnouts are not caused by our inner proletariats, but our inner *perverts*, exhausted from the superegotistic demand to endlessly stream our libido into the world. The cry of 'Father, don't you see I'm a selfie?' is at the core of burnouts, a desperate plea for help addressed at the superego upon confronting our own libido, which is at the same time an admission of guilt regarding our responsibilities. Burnouts betray a desire to leave all those data relations behind, to be finally able to stop taking selfies, using platforms, and being online—and yet, this is something our superego prevents us from facing. The popular solutions of unplugging, meditation, and other kinds of the so-called 'digital detoxing' are hence never really about leaving social media or tech behind altogether, but just reducing consumption, or taking a break so that we can eventually return to it. As such, they perpetuate the ideology of narcissism we have discussed earlier, to stay attached but without killing yourself or getting hysterical—to maintain good optics. Only we, the purveyors of libido, can save the world, because we are the sources of what the Market needs to manifest into a physical Other: data. The superego is the voice of incessant data provision: life must be turned into images, society into platforms.

But it is not enough that data is produced—it must also be able to reproduce itself on a faster and faster scale, fast enough and detailed enough to determine future behaviours of large numbers of people. A true hegemonic position needs to endlessly reproduce knowledge without effort—to produce self-reproducing knowledge, to write knowledge that knows how to write itself. The crucial apparatus of power has always been the apparatus of writing, but today, it requires the apparatus of *automated* writing. Code is today's predominant material substrate of power.

Flickering Fetishism

A proper response to capitalism always requires a detailed observation of the distribution of the material substrates of power. This term refers to objects used to discipline, inflict damage, or incite enjoyment upon one's life: tanks, waterboards, schools, CCTVs, sexual instruments, money, physical bodies, etc. The usage of these tools is fundamentally relational and socio-symbolic. This is how we reconcile our Marxist tradition with a more Foucauldian approach to power: what is often mistaken as power is in fact the concentration of material substrates of power. The concentration of military equipment can easily make for an authoritarian government or global threats of war and terrorism. The concentration of wealth and the racial, sexual, ableist, and other identity lines demarcating this concentration is the hallmark of an unjust society, breeding marginalisation of various groups and demonisation of the poor.

The concentration of code that serves data collection and ownership results in burnouts, anxieties, Alt-Right movements, antagonistic filter bubbles, and the epistemological crushing of marginalised narratives. This concentration of code legitimises itself through participatory play. It controls, shapes, and disciplines who we appear to be, with whom we ought to identify, to whom we ought to aspire, and how we should feel guilty that we are not yet a certain way. Psychopolitics is characterised by a lack of coercion, presenting itself as a freedom of options. Instead of fearing practices of capitalist control, we are delighted with them and dependent on them, and so we help perpetuate capitalism in its hegemonic position by providing data for their self-reproduction through code. This is what makes envisioning any real alternatives to capitalism so elusive in spite of how deep the discontent against it runs throughout society, and why we prefer to live in a mode of disavowal instead.

But psychopolitics has a structure, and it is by examining this structure that hope is to be found. We must first realise that no psychopolitical control will ever reach the core of the Subject. Its locus is instead the specular image, the flickering signifiers that are assembled in our stead, which the Market misrecognises as our true, desiring selves. This misrecognition is always disavowed, and in its place we find a constant, perverse reaffirmation of its own efficacy through our participation in its ludic social sphere. The assemblage of specular images as well as the design of the Market-affirming social relations rely on these flickering signifiers, for the most part esoteric in their layers of machine-to-machine communication.

Marxism claims that the relationship between people has been replaced by a relationship between objects. Today, the Real of social life itself is assigned a monetary value through its mediation by blinking pixels on a screen that mine our data in its depths. The relationship between people is replaced by a relationship between *images of people*. As we have analysed in the previous chapters, the anxiety of the Symbolic castration in online spaces has given rise to a plethora of online conflicts and discontents. In our attempts at sanitising neighbours and relationships, we subject everything to the cute gaze.

Following this logic to the extreme takes us back to Joe Goldberg, with whom we started this chapter. Isn't Joe's stalker behaviour, his voyeuristic obsession towards a totalising knowledge of his romantic prey, simply an obsession with the perfect selfie? As a stalker, Joe can only fall in love *through* social media. It is the specular image that he loves, his control over this image that he is obsessed with. This is precisely why Joe breaks down into a murderous rampage during moments where the perfection of the selfie begins to break—the woman is cheating, the friend is lying, and so on. An Other without otherness becomes impossible.

This violent tendency is structural. Most if not all conflicts revolve around the signifier. Throughout this book, we have illustrated how such violence manifests into misogyny, racism, ableism, and other forms of bigotry often associated with Right-wing movements. But we claim that such a tendency has seeped into the entire realm of politics and knows no spectrum. After all, do we not see a similar frustration from the Left when it sees its own image of the ideal progressive movement for the good of the many become cracked, e.g. in various conflicting strains of feminism, in transmedicalism, in debates surrounding Islam, or even when particular individuals seem to be following people who have not made the correct virtue signals? Such an obsession towards signifiers that detracts from forming a universal solidarity and instead causes us to become caught up in various internal debates in a futile attempt to sanitise ourselves seems to be characteristic of the Left today. Meanwhile, the Right becomes more and more monstrous and vocal in its ideas to eliminate particular groups of people from society.

From an explosion of identity politics to the obsession of bodies, extreme degrees of anxiety and antagonism revolve around one's online specular image and the images of others. Our task, then, is to resist these temptations and attempt to bring to light the further complexities and nuances within today's politics, and to how enjoyment, desire, and desperate cries for sexual recognition all come into play.

Chapter 6

Too Close, but not Close Enough: Politics and Sexuality in Times of the Alt-Right

The Over-proximity of Power

When the high-profile German judge Daniel Paul Schreber woke up one morning in 1893, he wished to engage in sexual intercourse with a woman. He felt alarmed by this thought because he experienced it as coming from somewhere outside of himself. He was convinced that a doctor, who had previously used hypnosis on him, had telepathically implanted the thought in him. In his psychotic state, he believed himself to be receptive to subliminal communication by others through sun-like 'rays', as he called them. This ultimately led to the fantasy that God was attempting to turn him into a woman.

Schreber is of immense significance for the history of psychoanalysis because he wrote about his experiences in a highly sophisticated and reflexive way. His memoir was famously interpreted by Freud, who argued that Schreber had repressed homosexual desires. Deleuze and Guattari critiqued Freud's interpretations and instead used the Schreber text as an expression of the manifestations of power in capitalism. For them, Schreber was a proto-fascist whose paranoia anticipated, and would have affirmed, the paranoia of the Nazi dictatorship under Hitler. Those points have been developed and advanced by Eric L. Santner, who argues that Schreber's 'breakdown and efforts at self-healing introduced him into the deepest structural layers of the historical impasses and conflicts that would provisionally culminate in the Nazi catastrophe' (Santner 1996, xi).

Santner interprets Schreber's paranoia as a manifestation of an over-proximity of power which chokes the Subject and gets all too near to their very core. The paranoia Schreber felt, as he himself wrote in his memoir (he had a second episode of mental illness just as he was appointed a presiding judge in the Saxony Supreme Court of Appeals), is only the individual manifestation of the Law, the social bond and wider structures that had been poisoned by conspiracy, anxiety, paranoia, and destruction. It was no coincidence that Schreber fell ill just when he was appointed as presiding judge and would come to embody the Law. Such perverse power structures that haunted him were states which would be heightened in Nazi Germany.

Schreber died in 1911, after being admitted to a state asylum for the third time. 'Among the symptoms reported in his chart are outbursts of laughter and screaming, periods of depressive stupor, suicidal gestures, poor sleep, and delusional ideas of his own decomposition and rotting,' writes Santner (ibid, 6). This is reminiscent of incels who often use the term *LDAR* when they discuss suicidal thoughts: *Lie Down And Rot*. They similarly cultivate outbursts of laughter which are overshadowed by depressive and psychotic elements. Santner argues that the feeling of rotting Schreber experienced was mirrored in 'a general sense of decay, degeneration, and enervation [that] were registered in fin-de-siècle social and cultural criticism' (ibid). This sense of decay would ultimately be appropriated by the Nazis and projected onto Jews, communists, gays and lesbians, people with disabilities, and others with 'differences'.

The Internet's Own Schreber

In 2009, US citizen Erik C. Estavillo sued tech giant Sony because he had been banned from the Playstation Network (PSN), an online network for multiplayer Playstation games. While playing *Resistance: Fall of Man*, he had allegedly used abusive language against other players. After a series of bans, his console was finally banned from the network altogether. In his self-published Kindle book, *The PSN Plaintiff: A Biography*

(2012), Estavillo notes that he was 'the first person in history to be punished by the fourth and final type of ban' (Estavillo 2012, 16). He felt that this ban was unsubstantiated and he had only behaved like many other players in the game.

He took Sony to court as he felt his First Amendment rights had been violated. Estavillo opted to represent himself as most lawyers he approached considered the case unwinnable or too insignificant to take on. Unsurprisingly, he lost the case. Sony argued that PSN was not part of the state and therefore First Amendment rights did not apply. This did not stop Estavillo from initiating lawsuits against Nintendo and Microsoft (because of bugs that impacted his gaming experiences), Blizzard (because characters allegedly walked too slowly in the game *World of Warcraft*), and the streaming platform Twitch (because female streamers caused him to furiously masturbate). Estavillo's case bears some resemblances to Schreber's, particularly in his reasoning for taking Sony to court because he felt singled out and haunted by an Other with absolute power.

Is Estavillo not the internet's own Schreber, a modern-day patient of the networked age? While we cannot make any substantial comments on his mental history, his writing exhibits a crisis of signifiers similar to the one which we have discussed in Chapter 2. He subsequently retreats into video games, a parallel universe where social relations and signifiers may seem more intact. It is thus all the more damaging to his sense of self when he is banned and the Symbolic is once again experienced as collapsing, penetrating, the Other too near, overshadowing his existence. 'The worst part of being banned was that I lost the ability to communicate and socialize with other people' (ibid, 16). Estavillo was cancelled. Those experiences provided him with a renewed agency, however, to take on the Other, a genuine belief that he could win and reassert his own Symbolic.

Like Schreber's, Estavillo's discontents are only symptomatic of the wider crises we find ourselves in. His fantasies are prophetic of social changes that would come to dominate the internet and wider political sphere from ca. 2014 onwards: Gamergate, incels, Trump, the Alt-Right, fake news, widespread conspiracy theories, the call to resist the mainstream. He embodies such attributes and feels persecuted by an Other who is too near.

More recently, Estavillo made headlines again as he decided to sue the streaming platform Twitch for $25 million in June 2020. Now also a self-proclaimed sex addict, court documents read that Twitch had 'extremely exacerbated his condition by displaying many sexually suggestive women streamers through Twitch's twisted programming and net code making it nearly impossible for the plaintiff to use Twitch without being exposed to such sexually suggestive content' (Ortega 2020, online). He called on Twitch to permanently ban a list of female streamers as they caused him to chronically masturbate while staying up long hours and staring at them. He even 'once ejaculated on his personal computer's monitor, causing it to short circuit and spark a fire that left his apartment in a blackout' (ibid).

While he was probably banned for all the correct reasons, he saw himself presented with a close yet intangible and unaccountable technostructure that embodied absolute power. He is the quintessential alienated Subject of Capitalism that seeks to subvert the Real gap in the Symbolic Order. The double standards he encounters (he is allegedly not allowed to swear online but rappers can do so in their songs, as he laments in his biography) are symptomatic of experiences we have all dealt with. His own private crisis is the same structural crisis we find ourselves in. When it comes to the specific sexual dimension of this case, Estavillo seems like a lonely porn-addicted geek who fails to see the female Twitch streamers as real people, like the other men we have discussed in the previous chapters. But is his sex addiction not symptomatic of the wider symbiotic, perverse sexual non-relationship we all have with the Other via devices, screens, Networked AI, and tech companies, where our desire for attention and recognition is, fundamentally, a desire for sexual recognition?

Sexual Recognition and the Law

While Estavillo sought to resist the Market, he did so by calling on the faculty of the Law. This echoes the wider themes we have discussed in this book: from the plea of the digital Subject, 'Father, don't you see I'm a selfie?' to the demands by incels that the state should provide them with partners qua legal statutes. All of these demands are addressed to the Law—they are desperate cries for sexual recognition by the Law itself. At a time where the rest of the Symbolic realm is so fundamentally shattered and fragile, the only stable agency, it seems, is the Law.

As we have discussed in the previous chapter, perversion has the ultimate desire to bring back the absolute force of the Law. This is a kind of Law that is fascist and knows no deliberation, lawyers, or juries—the Law of the Father; an absolute Law that has the power to validate the Subject once and for all and to protect them against any threat. Subjects feel, in different ways and to varying degrees, vulnerable and invisible, having given up on intersubjective relations and thus are seeking recognition once and for all by the Other. This desire for recognition is the desire for a knowledge to cover over the gap of the sexual non-relation at the core of the Subject; sexuality is what drives knowledge.

Zupančič writes, if:

sexuality is the drive of knowledge, it is not simply because we are curious about sex, or because we sublimate the lack of sex with a passion for knowledge. For the lack at stake is not a possible lack of sex, but a lack at the very heart of sex, or, more precisely, it concerns sex as the very structural incompleteness of being' (2017, 141).

The different Symbolic means of talking about sexuality that we have discussed in this book (selfies, memes, incels, Projekt Melody, up to Estavillo's lawsuits) are all attempts to create knowledge that masks the Real of sexuality. Yet such attempts are never complete. Something is always missing. The strongest authority that is thus called upon is the Law. Perhaps the instance of the Law can (or so it is hoped) fill the void, by handing down the missing signifier that will complete them — or, rather, by cancelling those who possess certain signifiers of difference.

Cancelling the Other

The late Mark Fisher famously wrote about the cancellation of the future; a feeling of being trapped in a state of limbo with no hope, vision, or change in sight that is today seized by reactionary and fascist forces. In a time where there is no present to hold on to, nihilism and irony are symptomatic responses to a crisis which fails to provide a vision for the future. This failure is a failure of the Left. In its preoccupation with infighting, debates around identity politics, and its own problems (sexism, misogyny, ableism, etc.), the Left has failed to stop the cancellation of the future that Fisher diagnosed. If anything, it has passionately accelerated it in a kind of all-on death drive that speedily races into a wall. In *Exiting the Vampire Castle* (2013), Fisher took the Left to task for its self-centred and -referential online wars which revolved around cancelling others. Since the publication of that text, Twitter's call-out, pile-on, and rage culture has only increased.

While we broadly agree with Fisher's diagnosis, we feel that he fell into a similar trap when he critiqued cancel culture—and this critical response was articulated by many upon the wider circulation of the *Vampire Castle* text: an essentialist response which foregrounds class rather than intersectionality. The Left, and many other groups and individuals, has demonstrated problematic behaviour when it comes to trans issues, women, or race, for example. There is nothing wrong with calling out particular behaviour, but—and we agree with Fisher and the many other critiques of cancel culture in this respect—the tone in which it happens is excessive and serves capital and big tech rather than emancipatory politics.

However, critiquing cancel culture only as an instance of moralism, essentialism, and hysteria functions along the same dynamics of cancel culture it seeks to critique. Cancelling cancel culture is not the solution. Cancel culture is symptomatic of a wider set of complexities that go beyond issues of free speech, oppressive behaviour, or political difference. In many instances, it is an expression of the desire for an otherless Other (see Chapter 4) and an erasure of conflict, debate, contradiction, ambivalence, and ambiguity.

Cancel culture and the weaponisation of free speech against it by the Far Right are in a sense the same instances of *jouissance* where essentialist stances are mobilised—either through cancelling and annihilating somebody on grounds of what they have allegedly said or done, or by vehemently rejecting cancel culture and advocating a holding onto of particular signifiers. Both moves eschew complexity in favour of clear narratives, constructing master signifiers to try and get rid of otherness altogether.

While the Left has been busy cancelling each other, the Alt-Right and its various strains emerged and weaponised some of the Left's foundations against them: singular struggles, identity politics, language games. They have been turned into ironic tropes that are more popular with many young people than the real struggles they signify—or, rather, parody. There may be no future, but unlike the Left, the Alt-Right and similar groups have provided the visual language for this cancelled future through racist memes and the like. While, much like the contemporary Left, the Alt-Right was at least partially born out of an emphasis of the visual (see Chapters 3 and 4), it managed to mobilise a vast troll army of online supporters. It is very easy to harness the general burnout and depression of our contemporary age into a potential for violence, and the Alt-Right have expertly done so in their focus on irony and nihilism. The future may be cancelled, but you can still post about it on Instagram, Reddit, and TikTok.

Nihilism and Irony: The Ultimate *Jouissance*

Much has been written about the generational differences between Boomers (people born between 1946 and 1964), Millennials (born between 1981 and 1996), and Generation Z (born between 1996 and the early 2000s). Generation Z has been described as nihilistic, pessimistic, collectivist, and interested in identity play. The strong use of irony and nihilism by the Alt-Right responds to an already existing sense of hopelessness across this generation. Unlike previous generations, Gen Z-ers were born into highly precarious times in which capitalism has failed to mask its own unproductivity, exploitation, and oppression. They then respond to our perverse culture with a sense of hopelessness and air their grievances on social media. Such grievances often take the form of complaints against the Other—in many cases the previous generations—for failing to provide the wealth and security that they are supposed to enjoy (Citarella 2019).

This gloomy celebration of no future is the ultimate *jouissance* for this generation. It goes hand-in-hand with a strong sense of vulnerability as we have discussed in relation to the selfie (Chapter 3). Other users become a perverse validator of the Subject's existence who both reinforce and shatter the Subject's confidence by endlessly validating them through likes and comments and at the same time repeating that this is all in vain and there is no future anyway. The Alt-Right, and its various more recent offshoots and sub-groups, provide narratives and an ideology which amplifies this form of *jouissance* and connects it to enemies (women, queers, people of colour, the state, the lockdown, climate change, etc.) that its mostly straight White male supporters can latch onto. The fantasies of general nihilism and hopelessness are responded to with ironic fantasies of phallic power which are both inherently defensive and powerful. When things get too heated, it can always be turned off. It was all a joke, after all, done 'for the *lulz*'.

Ultimately, nothing ever really needs to happen. While they do not deny the reality of climate change, for example, they are too exhausted by the mere thought of combating it. Furthermore, it is actually a source of *pleasure* for Gen Z-ers when they upload yet another list of grievances to the Other onto TikTok or chat about it on a Discord server, giving them a sense of pride and signalling hopelessness as a kind of moral virtue. While every generation revolts against the previous one, the collective curses, pleas, demands, and complaints of Generation Z are constitutive of their sense of identity. A witty post about the actual or impending economic, ecological, and sexual crises may be objectively true, but the potential for it to attract thousands of likes is the *objet a* icing on the cake.

On the more politically active end, one discovers that the arena has been turned into that of dissatisfied customer rants. The political is no longer a realm of true social change, but a domain of capitalist relations where concerns of citizenship are posed in the same manner as customer complaints (Han 2017). Citizens are merely frustrated users of the platform called nation-state, who have no choice but to participate in its functioning. Attempting to change the platform is futile and exhausting—but at least your customer complaints can be aired as a virtue, and your collective hopelessness can be celebrated together in a nice, Instagrammable coffee shop that will get you lots of likes; swipe right, maybe, and your sexual needs, too, can be fulfilled in a quick one-night stand without having to deal with that lame, cheesy thing called love. Hopelessness and irony, above all, provide a *safe space* in their promise—the relish of collective despair, the enjoyment of never being too disappointed ever again.

Is this not also the logic that more and more of us are adopting in the midst of the COVID-19 pandemic? Faced with a life-threatening disease of global proportions that halts much of the economy, bringing with it a future of extreme uncertainty, we still go on, with just a little bit of masks, social distancing, and increased frequency of hand-washing. The routines of life under capitalism must continue. The world is going downhill in many respects; as long as Instagram, Discord, and Twitter are still online, and TikTok and Tinder maybe, one might as well enjoy the ride.

Cancelling Desire

The rise of hook-up apps and websites like Tinder, Grindr, Bumble, OkCupid, and many others promise automated desire. They operate with an ideology that tells its users the sexual non-relation can be successfully covered over (e.g. with an ideal romantic relationship or no-strings-attached casual sex). Algorithms and matching mechanisms will bring the perfect sex partner, soulmate, friend with benefits, or life companion. This illusion pretty soon reveals itself as just that, as users cannot stop swiping even if (or especially when) they have numerous matches. The underlying mechanism fuels the desire to desire, to keep wanting. Desire itself becomes algorithmic, perhaps as it has always been. We treat matches as collections, our swiping often permeated with the *ennui* of pointless scrolling or grinding through a game we are no longer that interested in playing— surely, the perfect match lies just around the next swipe. While everyone is still using the platforms, nihilism kicks in. We know what we are doing and do it anyway.

This state of desire, somewhere torn between tech-savviness and old-fashioned neuroses, is illuminatingly pictured in the short story *Cat Person* by Kristen Roupenian, published in the New Yorker in December 2017. It went viral and was hailed as the first story of the #MeToo movement. It tells of Margot, a 20-year-old college student, who meets 34-year-old Robert, while she works at a cinema. 'Robert was cute. Not so cute that she would have, say, gone up to him at a party, but cute enough that she could have drummed up an imaginary crush on him if he'd sat across from her during a dull class' (2017, online). The two start exchanging flirtatious, funny, and ironic texts, and eventually go on a date which turns out to be rather awkward. They go back to Robert's place, and as they are about to have sex, Margot realises that she does not want to, but that it is somehow too late not to go through with it.

The story spoke to many readers about dating and sexual experiences. Its key scene depicts a sexual encounter in which Margot feels uncomfortable but goes ahead anyway because it would be too awkward and embarrassing to pull out of. Margot imagines herself as desired by the other, Robert, and takes a kind of narcissistic pleasure in this: 'He looked stunned and stupid with pleasure, like a milk-drunk baby, and she thought that maybe this was what she loved most about sex—a guy revealed like that' (Roupenian 2017, online). As they kiss, she imagines that Robert thinks about her as the perfect, flawless girl and she feels 'carried away by a fantasy of such pure ego that she could hardly admit even to herself that she was having it' (ibid). Roupenian continues:

> Margot sat on the bed while Robert took off his shirt and unbuckled his pants, pulling them down to his ankles before realizing that he was still wearing his shoes and bending over to untie them. Looking at him like that, so awkwardly bent, his belly thick and soft and covered with hair, Margot recoiled. But the thought of what it would take to stop what she had set in motion was overwhelming; it would require

an amount of tact and gentleness that she felt was impossible to summon. (Roupenian 2017, online)

Is this not the perfect description of the sexual non-relation, how it is shaped by conflicting desires, and what ultimately happens when fantasy becomes reality? Robert is ugly and terrible in bed, as Margot thinks. When she decides not to progress the texts and casual encounter into a serious relationship, Robert is hurt. The story ends with text messages he sends after seeing her at a bar:

"Hi Margot, I saw you out at the bar tonight. I know you said not to text you but I just wanted to say you looked really pretty. I hope you're doing well!"

"I know I shouldnt say this but I really miss you"

"Hey maybe I don't have the right to ask but I just wish youd tell me what it is I did wrog"

"*wrong"

"I felt like we had a real connection did you not feel that way or…"

"Maybe I was too old for u or maybe you liked someone else"

"Is that guy you were with tonight your boyfriend"

"???"

"Or is he just some guy you are fucking"

"Sorry"

"When u laguehd when I asked if you were a virgin was it because youd fucked so many guys"

"Are you fucking that guy right now"

"Are you"

"Are you"

"Are you"

"Answer me"

"Whore." (Roupenian 2017, online)

Such a cascade of messages that turn from nonchalant to abusive in a matter of minutes is all too well-known for many women on the internet. This story can be read as another instance of heteropessimism, the never-ending cruelty of desire, the inability to traverse the fantasy, or the avoidance of real communication between Margot and Robert. Margot texts Robert to stop contacting her as she is not interested in him, and eventually resorts to 'ghosting' him. This speaks to the wider dynamics of romantic life as a database in today's culture—if Margot's life was a platform, Robert was being cancelled.

Sanitising the Database

Cat Person led to an outpouring of reactions, interpretations, and written responses. Like any good text, readers could interpret it according to their own fantasies and see what they wanted to see in it. This was a deliberate move on the part of Roupenian, who kept the characters in *Cat Person* and her follow-up *You Know You Want This* anthology of short stories deliberately vague. 'It doesn't really matter who plays victim or abuser, desirer or desiree, since these operate according to their own self-propelling logic, like deep-learning algorithms chewing up input data,' writes Park MacDougald (2019, online). In today's culture, individuals have become mere data points that periodically intersect. As such, Roupenian is the perfect chronicler of our times of anonymity, sexual alienation, surveillance, and data. She narrates her stories with a tone of flatness and nihilism which echoes the wider cultural-political ambience of pessimism and defeatism we have discussed. This makes *Cat Person* a political story, on top of the themes of consent and misogyny. Sex has become data-driven and organised around capitalist accumulation.

Nothing highlights the contemporary form of data-driven sex better than Tinder. The journalist Nancy Jo Sales talked to

Tinder users about what she calls the 'dating apocalypse' and writes:

> With these dating apps, he says, 'you're always sort of prowling. You could talk to two or three girls at a bar and pick the best one, or you can swipe a couple hundred people a day—the sample size is so much larger. It's setting up two or three Tinder dates a week and, chances are, sleeping with all of them, so you could rack up 100 girls you've slept with in a year.' (Sales 2015, online)

No need to know the other. '"Ukrainian," Alex confirms. "She works at—" He says the name of a high-end art auction house. Asked what these women are like, he shrugs. "I could offer a résumé, but that's about it...Works at J. Crew; senior at Parsons; junior at Pace; works in finance..."' (Sales 2015, online), as Alex, a male Tinder user who works in finance, puts it. Hook-up apps present the perversity of capitalism gone full circle where Subjects are not only categorised and tracked by Big Data analytics but themselves mimic a logic of algorithmic surveillance and refer to themselves and others in categories. There is an endless potential surplus of matches.

Ultimately, desire is shown as dead and flat in *Cat Person*. The two bodies cancel each other out. Rather than just seeing this as a normal occurrence because Robert and Margot are not 'compatible', it reveals a sense of pointlessness where an empathic form of relating that acknowledges differences is completely absent. The characters have no real desire to discover the other person. This speaks to many of us today who rely on technology for our sexual relationships. Technology both mediates and severs actual connections between people because they can potentially lead to loss. The prospects of 'cancelling', 'ghosting', 'orbiting' (prolonged spying on someone via social media), 'breadcrumbing' (keeping someone interested without wanting to commit to a full relationship), 'cushioning' (keeping a single person in flirtatious contact while being in a relationship; if the relationship breaks down, the single person is instantly available to 'cushion' the breakup), and many other terms to describe contemporary forms of romantic relating are so appealing because they uphold a fantasy in which disappointment, pain, and anxiety do not exist.

This is also how we should read cancel culture today. As a practice, it is only made possible by the logic of the database— what is cancel culture if not a normalising of the methodical removal of connections from a database, a collective ghosting of particular individuals? While it is true that we must oppose those who deliberately harass others, trigger trauma, and commit various kinds of hate-motivated atrocities, we must be critical of how we frame such issues. All too often, can we not see members of the Left frantically swiping left and right regarding who should be allowed to match into the Leftist political sphere? Solidarity goes out the window as movements become more exclusionary rather than inclusive.

Just like Margot, we desire a sanitised space, a space suspended in time where we could relive the narcissistic enjoyment of making other people 'stunned and stupid with pleasure' (e.g. via getting retweets of our enraged takes) without having to deal with the recoil of over-proximity. Robert, illustrating the sadly prototypical reaction of contemporary masculinity, displaces the cause of such a recoil first into himself (he did something wrong, he was too old, etc.) then quickly, to protect his ego, into her (she was a whore). In turn, this justifies Margot's decision— Robert was abusive, after all, and it was fortunate that Margot got rid of him.

While we must assert the importance of a safe space and not undermine the need of individuals with certain traumatic experiences to avoid certain situations and particular individuals, we must also acknowledge that prolonged avoidance without ever dealing with the root cause of the problem is never the proper approach. Psychoanalysis teaches us that what must be questioned is the structure by which said individuals invest their emotional energy and how such investments lead to psychological suffering. Just like Margot and Robert's dynamic, cancel culture relies on displacing toxicity into the other being cancelled and takes the often reactionary backlash as a justification that they have always deserved cancellation. What is seemingly unthinkable for today's Margots and Roberts across the political spectrum is the inherent impossibility of a sanitised database—that the sexual, the political, and in fact every facet of the Symbolic itself will always bring with it an unbearable otherness. Antagonism and the impossibility of true relationships are inscribed in the logic of the database as a structure that portrays one's life as a platform and one's purpose as a collection—of experiences, sexual partners, and so on.

Technology offers the false promise of living out these dreams in a sanitised manner. Just like contemporary dating, cancel culture and the wider realms of politics wish for a form of society in which disappointment, pain, and anxiety do not exist. While perhaps naive, such a fantasy is not inherently bad. However, the way in which said fantasy is approached through technology—the methodical removal of particular individuals from a database in order to create a sanitised experience—is problematic. A narrative in which the world's problems can be solved by removing certain people from existence? We have a very familiar name for it.

The Promise of the Fascist Phallus

It is no coincidence that the form of perverse relating via hook-up apps that we discussed comes at a cultural moment in which politics are at a crossroads: fascism or an alternative.

Of course, actual fascism in practice goes much further than cancel culture in its annihilation of differences, and we do not intend to undermine its horrors by equating it to banal dating apps or rage threads on Twitter. However, a structural parallel can nonetheless be drawn. Both are animated by a promise of phallic power to those who feel disaffected, powerless, or left behind. We live in a culture that promises an Other without otherness, be it via Tinder or fascist ideology. Fascism promises an Other who can recognise my desires and is exactly like me, a replica of myself that destroys all contradiction, ambiguity, and any feared or 'different' others. Albeit in a far more benign form, dating apps operate with a similar logic in their core as they break other users into segments, signifiers, images, and data, in order to fulfil a promise that we can easily get rid of them for good if we find them unbearable or unattractive. This logic is coded into the design of dating apps and becomes the Law for its users.

While the prospect of escaping potentially problematic relationships from early on has undoubtedly saved many people from various horrors they may have had to endure otherwise—and, conversely, healthy relationships have been formed by many couples who met through the algorithm of dating apps—we nonetheless maintain that the phallic promises of this form of relating contains an inherent violence: the Subject is supposed to act like a dictator who can find a cleansed Other. Of course, unlike fascism proper, Tinder in its reciprocal relationality erases the unbalanced oppressor/ oppressed relation. Both Subjects need to swipe right in order to match. In Tinder's competitor Bumble, women are required to make the first move, although ultimately it comes down to a similar scenario. Their desires allegedly perfectly mirror each other as a truly objective, machinic form of libidinal relating is enabled through their unity. Users exploit each other in their desires for a surface-like connection; both embody a phallic subjectivity. Whereas the selfie expresses a naked vulnerability of the Subject who offers themself to the Other (see Chapter 3), hook-up apps promise an end to this vulnerability through sanitised relations. Subjects behave like specular images (see Chapter 5) and embody their narcissistic self-images.

Ultimately, the (unconscious) wish for many users is to destroy the other after sex so that any reminder of them is wiped out; they are erased in their fantasies so that they can start all over again without the baggage of love, embarrassment, or other complicated feelings. Can we not read the expressions which the individuals in Sales' *Vanity Fair* article use to describe Tinder as symbolic acts of killing? 'Tinder is fast and easy, boom-boom-boom, swipe,' 'Hit it and quit it,' '"It's like ordering Seamless,"' says Dan, the investment banker, referring to the online food-delivery service. "But you're ordering a person."' (Sales 2015, online). Tinder users hunt for *cuteness*, as it were, for a sanitised other *so cute you could almost eat them*. And when cuteness gets overbearing in its proximity, all you need to do is unmatch. No wonder many sexual encounters today are described as 'creepy'. It's not the person—it's simply the distance. In our subjective core, every one of us is creepy, even to ourselves, and we know it very well. Hook-up apps, ghosting practices, and cancel culture amount to the fantasy that perhaps creepiness does not belong to us, and the promise that we can remove it from our lives by cancelling particular individuals.

Against Sanitisation

In a society of cute database animals, creepiness must be cancelled. This fantasy of phallic relations comes to reveal itself in the moments when bodies enter into sensual relations. Men in particular seem to feel the pressure to fulfil the fantasy of the omnipotent phallic Other. '"It would be great if they could just have the ability to perform and not come in two seconds,"' says Rebecca' (Sales 2015, online). Erectile dysfunctions and 'performance anxiety' are on the rise in young men and experts cannot fully explain why (Kale 2018). As one of the women Sales interviewed puts it: 'A lot of guys are lacking in that department' (Sales 2015, online). The Real always returns to the sexual non-relation and disrupts the Imaginary—cuteness always turns creepy. Tinder users know that they are trapped in a repetitive circuit of desire and speak about it with a playful, ironic pseudo-detachment to mask the lack. They know that they might suffer or even be abused as a result of a Tinder date, yet carry on—it's too late to pull out of the sexual culture.

Our political situation today can also be read as a reactionary politics against creepiness. The Left falls prey to the database logic and engages in the promise of cancel culture to delete creepy differences from within and without their own platform, thus finding themselves in an endless cycle of internal squabble. The Right displaces creepiness onto particular groups of people—people of colour, feminists, queers, fat people, disabled people, immigrants, and others—to violently assert a monolithic form of supremacy. Those of us not otherwise engaged are too exhausted, choosing instead to host a pity party celebrating the loss of a future with drinks and casual sex, ghosting, and unmatching whenever things get too overwhelming.

One of the reasons we arrived at the situation we are in today is that the Right have appropriated so many master signifiers in the political sphere ('free speech', 'political correctness', 'being offended', etc.). They filled them with their own meaning as many Liberals and Leftists watched from the sidelines, not knowing how or choosing not to intervene. Of course, this can partly be explained through cancel culture and the strong conviction of many people that one should not debate or engage with the Far Right. While the recent alarming rise of fascism did more to unify the Left than previous developments, an intersectional coalition has yet to be formed. This can be exemplified by the Sanders and Warren supporters in the US who failed to come together, for example, or the various disagreements regarding whether or not the Left should vote.

In the future, platforms will seek to exert more control over the limits of freedom of speech. Recent Twitter bannings of high-profile Far Right and Alt-Right figures and Reddit's tightened moderation policy which led to the banning of e.g. r/The_Donald in July 2020 exemplify this. This means that fascist tactics and subcultures will both move back to fringe communities and platforms (e.g. 4chan, Gab, Parler, etc.) and be forced to adopt new tactics to influence the mainstream platforms and recruit followers. On the other hand, we also should not forget that many of the influential tech giants, e.g. Facebook, PayPal, Palantir, and ClearView AI, are systematically funded and partially controlled by individuals with a clear leaning to the Far Right (see e.g. Schwarz & Biddle 2019 on Mark Zuckerberg's dinners with Far Right figures or O'Brien 2020 for a discussion of ClearView AI).

The online war over signifiers will continue, and with it, increased misogyny and male fragility. We live in 'a culture that scorns weakness and punishes vulnerability, especially among men,' as Rachel O'Neill (2018, 213) writes. Tinder is just one example of this erasure of weakness in favour of surface appearances and specular images. To be weak is to be creepy, and the price to pay is being banned for life, swiped left, unmatched, ghosted. Those who receive this treatment—such as incels, Estavillo, or Robert—then resort to rebelling against women. This violence in turn gets them cancelled, eliminated from participation in various social spheres, which pushes them to cry out louder for sexual recognition, for phallic efficacy. They turn to the Alt-Right where they find a home for their rage and hatred, or wallow in collective despair as they flaunt their hopelessness as the new moral virtue.

All of these are conducted, of course, 'for the *lulz*'. For it is in the *lulz* of the Other that we find comfort: despair, irony, nihilism, casual racism, casual misogyny, casual self-objectification for endless swipes, casual exhibition of firearms amid half-joking cries for a new civil war. The failure of the database is at the same time a promise that it will get better, or perhaps more tolerable, if you could align yourself with its Law, for its *lulz*.

Nonetheless, we must not give in to hopelessness. The Black Lives Matter movement that started in 2013 and found its expression during the summer of 2020 is pregnant with revolutionary energy. It shows a Leftist movement going out of its usual dreary cancellations towards a sanitised space and truly fighting for a future. The radical movement not only has a clear message and strategy, but it managed to establish particular meanings and wider discourses (e.g. about anti-racism, decolonisation, and misogyny) via a universality of human suffering that can be accessed through the Black experience. This is why critics of BLM that acknowledge police violence but refuse to make it a racial issue completely miss the point—the movement precisely *has* to be framed as a racial issue in order to show the intersectionality and deep-rooted history of racial struggles. The supportive actions of K-Pop fans whom we have discussed in Chapter 3 are an example of discursive and visual tactics that also point towards this direction of solidarity across racial borders.

All in all, the movement resists the temptation of cute displays of multicultural identities where diversity is treated as a sanitised collection of text and images. Rather, it asserts the full historical weight of Blacks being treated as creepy—subhumans, rapists, criminals, and so on—and fights for a way out of this centuries-long legacy of racism. By doing so, it rejects the ideologies of political correctness that, as Žižek (2019) put it, position Whiteness as a universalist background (usually via a self-flagellating White guilt) while the experiences of people of colour are seen as particular expressions to be pitied, coddled, and celebrated like children. While they are not mutually exclusive—supporting BLM is the politically correct thing to do—the movement must always be posed as a challenge to structural racism supported by institutions of criminalisation *in spite* of political correctness—an assertion that Blacks, and other people of colour and minorities alike, do not need incessant White apology and bleeding-heart protection, and must instead be able to claim their own narratives and determine their own destinies.

Ultimately, the war must be fought in solidarity across all lines of struggles. Already the indigenous people of West Papua are fighting under the BLM banner to highlight their own oppression under Indonesia's prolonged military occupation of the area (Firdaus 2020; Varagur 2020). Movements like these tell us that in spite of all the irony and desperate laughter permeating the online sphere, hope is yet to be found.

Conclusion

Event Horizon

Beyond Language, into Topology

Today life is seen not only as a tool of production but as a mine for data production that can generate more wealth which the majority of the world will remain unable to access. With the myth of innovation and providing value to society, with seductive hooks and perverse playfulness, with promises of sexual recognition once and for all, we seem to have all collectively accepted such modes of life and particular images of the future as the best ones possible. And yet, anxieties, burnouts, depression, as well as rage and hatred, flare up with increasing frequency.

The Discourse of Capitalism, totalising in its infinite loop, has subsumed all meaning into its logic of relentless consumption, so much so that all attempts at erecting new quilting points get inextricably caught up in its web. Its very design presents a fundamental epistemic injustice, as distribution of wealth is also distribution of the means of knowledge production, pushing marginalised communities further away and only integrating them once they can become a source of profit for the owners of capital. It can only do so through the creation and sharpening of social antagonisms in the name of online engagement, positioning it as the engine of the attention economy. As such, it is an economy that functions on a sustained reproduction of a shared hatred of the Other's *jouissance*.

In this kind of economy, the over-proximate Other always seems to have better access to *jouissance* than we do. Stacy and Chad for the incels, Chris-chan for the trolls, Margot for Robert, and many other people for us always seem to have a more genuine, authentic relationship between their physical bodies and digital lives. The non-existence of the sexual relationship is internalised as a failure of self-commodification instead of an inherent feature of subjectivity.

However discontented we are, attempts at productive debates seem to always falter as quickly as they start. What was once a productive discussion on actual, critical issues degenerates into an inwards-facing impotence of who can claim a higher moral ground as individuals flame and cancel each other to cover over the lack in the Other (e.g. the failure for true social change). While the Left is plagued with such a disease, the Right drifts further and further into terrorism, mass shootings, and calls for an armed civil war, all tinged with racial supremacy and gender-based violence. New master signifiers that seem to resist capitalist ideology end up turning stale, inefficient, and ineffective against its infinite regime.

But is the fact that the efficacy of the master signifier seems to keep slipping away really something we must keep on lamenting? If no single banner of movement is capable of tackling the multiplicity of pathologies within capitalism, perhaps it is because *names as such* are no longer enough once the circle of epistemology is broken. Flickering signifiers blink in and out of existence on our screens, but perhaps they are just that—flickering, unstable, unreliable, slipping away beneath our fingers like the skin of a fruit. The perverse nature of capitalism often veers into symptoms very similar to those of psychosis. What must one do in the face of such madness?

The Playful Event

In a Žižekian manner, perhaps we can say that what we need is a new symptom for our times. But it would do us no good to take this at face value and insist on new master signifiers, else we would end up right back where we started in their ultimate inefficacy. Rather, we should aim for a new *sinthome*—a new topological organisation of *jouissance* that does not call for a linguistic interpretation but simply ties together the consistency of the Real-Symbolic-Imaginary ternary in the age of flickering signifiers.

We propose a reading of the Badiouian (2006) Event as the birth of a new *sinthome*. Ruptured as such, the decision to force towards a new set theoretical universe with militant fidelity should be understood as a *topological* movement, a reorganisation of the way Subjects access their *jouissance*—not necessarily by name, at least not at first, but always by a *sinthome*. It is not unlike *Finnegans Wake*, except that in this new universe, people actually understand what Joyce is writing about.

A primary reason that we are so addicted to social media and technology is because it is fun. It provides a delightful way to socialise and form connections, as well as the instantaneous feedback loop that manifests the Other into really existing numbers, metrics, and other UX elements on screen. We willingly trade privacy for comfort, not because we are lazy and stupid but simply because it is in accordance to the pleasure principle. Psychopolitics works on our specular image, but it does so very effectively, rewarding us with the power to control and build upon our imaginary selves as no less than a lifelong project through entrepreneurship and self-branding. Furthermore, we witness this functioning effectively for some people, who generate vast amounts of wealth by becoming the so-called 'influencers' of social media.

To erect any hope of a social structure that may outlast capitalism as such, we must conceive of one that is, first and foremost, *fun*. Everyone must be excited, delighted, even seduced into taking part in the new society, for it is delightful, abundant with hitherto unforeseen opportunities. Much of the appeal of Black Lives Matter lies in these very possibilities, that Blacks and other marginalised communities may start to invent their own future. A social structure is an organisation of *jouissance*, and it is the Subjects' enjoyment that must take centre stage of consideration when thinking of new possibilities. And since forward is the only possible direction, it is technology that we must seize for such an invention.

It is perhaps strange for a book that is so critical of technology to advocate a return to it. We should re-emphasise, however, that what we have been criticising throughout the book is not technology as such, but rather its configurations within the capitalist framework. We must be careful not to throw the baby out with the bathwater. While the black-boxing of mechanisms that lie beyond the screen and the controller is always suspect to ideological manipulation, we nonetheless maintain that a playful use of technology is a potential sphere when it comes to the reorganisation of *jouissance*.

Erotic, Panic

What will love and sexuality of the future look like? In response to debates on pornography and sexual oppression among Second Wave feminists, the Black lesbian writer and activist Audre Lorde (1984) called for a new conceptualisation and use of the erotic. For Lorde, the erotic stands for a source of women's power that can be uncoupled from sexuality, and furthermore, diametrically opposed to pornography. The erotic embodies feminine desire and power regardless of particular signifiers that denote sexual identity and orientation. It should not be regarded as synonymous with particular displays of female inferiority or superiority, as those are only oppressive manifestations of patriarchy. Erotically empowered women are dangerous, and for that reason, writes Lorde, forces of oppression have divorced the erotic from all spheres of life apart from sexuality. It is instead presented in a corrupt, distorted manner as pornography, which is its opposite in so far as pornography is concerned with 'sensation without feeling' (ibid, 54) as opposed to a deep, spiritual, inner power source.

Today, almost 40 years after Lorde's essay was published,

we can see quite clearly that feelings, too, have become a site of control, taken apart and collected via social media, self-entrepreneurship, practices of meditation, and so on. Depth is a fiction written by the master signifier, and any notion of an inner spirituality is bound to become a tool of ideology. But we propose a different reading of Lorde's ideas. What if, instead of rediscovering a true, spiritual plane of the erotic, we affirm the erotic as *purely fictional*? Can we not decisively *invent* the erotic as something radically new? Perhaps the solution is not to rediscover an inner spirituality and mend its divorce with other spheres of life, but precisely to divorce it entirely from everything else.

Capitalism as such has entirely corrupted and severed all forms of deep spirituality, rendering it impossible—but the hole that it covers over remains. This is the sexual non-relation, the structural negativity that defines the Subject as such, an ontological parasite whose existence depends on the failure of ontology. It is from this subjective place that we are free to invent the erotic.

Consider Richard Siken's poetry:

Tell me about the dream where we pull the bodies out of the lake
and dress them in warm clothes again.
How it was late, and no one could sleep, the horses running
until they forget that they are horses.
It's not like a tree where the roots have to end somewhere,
it's more like a song on a policeman's radio,
how we rolled up the carpet so we could dance, and the days
were bright red, and every time we kissed there was another apple
to slice into pieces.
Look at the light through the windowpane. That means it's noon,
*   that means*
we're inconsolable.
Tell me how all this, and love too, will ruin us.

These, our bodies, possessed by light.
Tell me we'll never get used to it.
(*Scheherazade*; Siken 2005, 3)

The poem asks the Other to be complicit in its surreal enunciation: the dream of comforting dead bodies, a loss of identity in an animalistic forward thrust. It rhymes not on the level of the signifier but of the *semblant*: the red of a carpet, the red of the day, the red of apples, the red of lips—and implicitly, perhaps, the red of blood—all organising a *jouissance* (dancing, kissing, eating, sin) under the light of a ruinous love. The poem is a *sinthome* without the need for interpretation, offering no master signifier. There is the idea of love, but it is external and senseless. Poet and critic Louise Glück writes that it portrays 'loss as enacted, not implicit, event' (Glück in Siken 2005, xi).

'This is a book about panic,' she writes of *Crush*, the collection in which the poem appears. 'The speaker is never outside of it long enough to differentiate panic from other states' (ibid, vii). Siken thus creates a world where 'panic is a synonym for being' (ibid.)—in other words, a world in which being itself is disrupted, thus creating panic as a primary mode of subjectivity. When Badiou (2005) writes of terror apropos of the ontological rupture of the Event (revolutionary terror, etc.), was he not speaking precisely of this condition? Compare how Lorde writes of the erotic as a form of sensuality: 'those physical, emotional, and psychic expressions of what is deepest and strongest and richest within each of us, being shared: the passions of love, in its deepest meanings' (Lorde 1984, 56). When we take this to the extreme, do we not arrive at a world of panic? We can thus draw a substantive parallel between the two conceptions, one seen as an immanent trajectory from a chaotic core, the other written precisely *from the inside*, in a state of Being caught in the terror of the Event.

Siken's poetry shows 'a fusion of the erotic and the life-threatening' (Glück in Siken 2005, xi). It comes from a point of reckless decision that is, against all better judgement, already decided, and thus inescapable. It is an impossible invention, external and ruinous yet something the Subject cannot help but enact through deciding an undecidable. Here, we move beyond the dynamics of dis/inhibition—nothing is dammed up; desire is not a stream, and has never been one. Rather, it is 'a well of replenishing and provocative force to the woman who does not fear its revelation, nor succumb to the belief that sensation is enough' (Lorde 1984, 53). It is a well also in the sense that it has the structure of a hole—but it is a negativity that nonetheless becomes our source of energy.

For Siken, while replenishing, this well is also threatening, murderous:

> ...Here are the illuminated
> cities at the center of me, and here is the center
> of me, which is a lake, which is a well that we
> can drink from, but I can't go through with it.
> I just don't want to die anymore.
> (Saying Your Names; Siken 2005, 36)

It is quite telling that this realisation comes at the very end of a poem about names—a poem that, according to Glück, 'can't stop' (2005, vii) in its incessant enunciation of the fleeting ('the names of flowers that open only once', 33), the unreliable ('names I called you behind your back', 33), pregnant with *jouissance* ('names like pain cries', 34). Confronted with the failure of naming, one moves to the circular enjoyment of its enunciation, before finally arriving at the well at the centre of the Subject. The speaker does not want to die because the revelation of desire as such is threatening, and, as evident in the other poems in *Crush*, the speaker always wants to succumb to the belief that sensation alone is enough—life is unbearable otherwise, caught in the inchoate catastrophe of love.

In Siken's lines one finds the failure of meaning in the face of the erotic drive, and the traumatic emptiness at the core of subjectivity. But perhaps most fundamentally, one finds the importance of a radical decision that grounds the invention of the erotic:

> ... *This is where the evening*
> *splits in half, Henry, love or death. Grab an end, pull hard,*
> *and make a wish.*
> (*Wishbone*; Siken 2005, 41)

Beyond the Sexual Non-Relation

We are here not trying to romanticise panic as a prolonged state of eroticism. Revolutionary terror, after all, must end, as we settle into a universe with a new organisation of *jouissance*. Rather, what we are attempting to do is to affirm the traumatic nature of the sexual non-relation as the necessary starting point to invent a new, asexual erotics. 'The great task has been to infuse clarity with the passionate ferment of the inchoate,' writes Glück (2005, xii). Thus, like Siken's poetry, the erotic is a means to make sense of the inchoate—or as Lorde put it, 'a measure between the beginnings of our sense of self and the chaos of our strongest feelings' (1984, 53). The erotic should be understood as a radical invention within this panic—not as any futile attempt to deny our inconsistent subjectivity, cover over the gap of the Other, or displace lack into a certain group within society, but to affirm the messy chaos within our being as such and work from it. It is at once obsessive, vulnerable, and feminine.

As such, the erotic functions as a relationality between Subjects; it is 'the sharing of joy' (Lorde 1984, 56), be it physical, intellectual, emotional, or psychic. This relationality entails an 'understanding much of what is not shared between them, and lessens the threat of their difference' (ibid). This point is important. The erotic does not attempt to make meaning out of every little gesture. It resists interpretation, sacrifice, heroism, and maintains a space for misunderstanding and things not shared; it acknowledges nonsensicality and contradiction and embraces the impossibility of speaking the whole truth. Differences no longer become a threat as homophily becomes anachronistic, obsolete. Relationships are formed neither like the roots of a tree nor like rhizomatic networks, but like a song on a policeman's radio: messy, fleeting, interrupted, but ever-present.

The erotic manifests in practices like dancing, playing with a pet, reading a good book, as well as experiences such as epiphany, gender euphoria, and class solidarity, among others. Emma Goldman's famous quote, 'If I can't dance to it, it's not my revolution,' takes on a new significance: the panic-inducing dark night of the Event must be followed by an erotic dawn of a new life. Embracing the erotic grounds the realisation that, for all the exploitation that I have endured, my life should be filled by joy. I am capable of receiving and giving joy, of inventing and sharing joy, not in spite of my lack and inconsistencies, not in spite of my alienation and the erasure of all of my spiritual and ethnic roots, but precisely because of them. This joy is different from the fleeting pleasures of continuous posting, bottomless consumption, and endless collection motivated by the capitalist superego, in so far as these rely on master signifiers of the market and function on guilt and ennui. Rather, it is the joy of discovery, the joy of invention, the joy of hope for radical possibilities of life we never knew we had.

In capitalism, the situation is admittedly much more complex. Comedy, memes, and various kinds of visual tactics as well as all manners of enjoyment have been subsumed under its machine. But the dominant regime is clear: all joy, as it were, is best practised with an ironic distance, laughed at with the strict morality of despair. The challenge of the erotic is thus to bring new configurations of joy that shed light on new hopes for a possible world. When hopelessness is a moral virtue, the erotic, as it does, strives to be immoral.

While Lorde advocated the use of the erotic specifically as a means of empowerment for queer people of colour, we believe we must extend it as a universal revolutionary practice. An asexual erotics, as it has recently been further developed by Ela Przybylo (2019), means acknowledging and utilising affect and desire for means that go beyond the sexual. As Lorde writes:

> [A]llowing that power to inform and illuminate our actions upon the world around us, then we begin to be responsible to ourselves in the deepest sense. For as we begin to recognize our deepest feelings, we begin to give up, of necessity, being satisfied with suffering and self-negation, and with the numbness which so often seems like their only alternative in our society. [...] The need for sharing deep feeling is a human need. But within the European-American tradition, this need is satisfied by certain proscribed erotic comings-together. These occasions are almost always characterized by a simultaneous looking away [...]. (Lorde 1984, 57-58)

This 'mutual coming together in looking away' Lorde writes of is characteristic of sexuality. After all, is it not just another phrase for attempts to cover over the sexual non-relation, for example by incels' fantasies, by pornography, and to a much subtler degree by our use of selfies? This is where we find a possible limit to earlier forms of psychoanalytic practice, in so far as it continues to rely on developing new master signifiers to traverse the fantasy that covers over this lack. Fortunately, as we have hinted at, we believe Lacan himself already points towards the direction of this impasse as he moves beyond linguistics into the realm of topology from 1975 onwards—Lacan of the *sinthome*, not of the symptom. Linguistics forces us to look away as it covers the abyss with the myth of the efficacy of the master signifier. Topology allows us to stop looking away—a move that, of course, brings us into panic. In the face of this inchoate terror, in place of a master signifier, we argue for an erotics of profound empathy as we stare into the abyss. In this manner, we move beyond the individual Lacanian Subject into the proper collective Subject of the Event—only this time, the need for a name is supplanted by an understanding of what cannot be shared.

A Tired, Doubtful Struggle

Complacency to suffering—perhaps best embodied by what Badiou (2005) calls the Obscure Subject, defined by their bitter, cynical lamentation of the present—is precisely what the erotic wages a war against. Critical race theorist Mari Matsuda— whose writings are full of erotic sensibilities in this precise sense—illustrates this affect very well:

> Have you ever fallen in love? Have you ever looked at someone's back and suddenly realized you want to put your hand on their back and bring everything good upon them— keep them safe, keep them in a circle of joy, make cruelty stay far, far away? (Matsuda 2005, 202)

It is also in this sense that we can arrive at a non-violent understanding of the cute. Uncoupling the cute from its surface-level flatness, one comes to a different appreciation of the cute other: vulnerability, femininity, care. This is not the performative cuteness of selfies or pornographic anime characters. Rather, this is the cuteness of a child, of small animals, markedly different in that the emotion is grounded in panic and doubt: Will I really be able to take care of this creature, so complex, so full of life? Am I good enough to keep them from harm? In this form, the oppressive dimension of consumerism, which capitalism does its best to get us to enact (i.e. taking care of a child means giving them a lot of toys, gadgets, screen time, etc.), is completely cast aside. Freed from its consumerist injunctions, the appreciation of cuteness becomes a trembling at the weight of responsibility to care for and nurture, not unlike a trembling one experiences at great heights, borne of the realisation that one could, at any time, destroy a life so full of potential.

The use of the erotic as a revolutionary practice means that the romanticism and heroism of struggle, too, is stripped away in favour of a less masculinist approach that takes into account its messy, vulnerable, and inconsistent aspects. It neither seeks for signs of betrayal nor becomes cynical in tolerating betrayals. It is not self-righteous but self-aware, and weary, in constant doubt of itself.

The erotic is the depth of feelings and emotion that follow the panic of the Event. It attempts to push forward in the fight against pain and suffering. But it is not a joyous celebration of vitalist positivity. Rather, it is an acknowledgement of the shared experience of our traumatic subjective core. It tries to make sense of the inchoate, and as such is marked by self-doubt. Its militant fidelity, to use Badiou's term, is not characterised by an unflinching faith, but in the fact that there is simply no other choice: the alternative has become intolerable. The only choice is between love or death.

How the erotic, and love, and sexuality will configure themselves in the future is something we cannot know. Whether or for how long the institution of marriage will stand into the future, for example, or how practices of monogamy and polyamory will evolve, or how the circulation of sexual images will be negotiated in a society increasingly aware of exploitation are all questions to which we do not have the answer. Nonetheless, Mari Matsuda is once again enlightening in her two principles of liberation struggles:

1. Any argument that takes as a starting point the limits of liberation constructed by the perceived power of the oppressor is suspect.
2. Any argument that starts with a utopian vision of true, substantive equality for all human beings must stay on the table regardless of what interim choice is made. (Matsuda 2005, 186-187)

Now we can come back to our emphasis of the importance of the technological and the playful to build spaces of possibilities — this time with guidelines as to what principles we can utilise to ground our explorations. It is from these considerations that we can begin to posit three points of imagination in considering an alternative future.

A New Universe

How will we live when our digital social spaces are not defined by rage against the Other but by playful creative interactions which serve as our own means of production, where facilities for the common good are free and participation in the social fabric brings us wealth?

We end this book by posing the following questions:

1. The Epistemic Question: How can we enable access to and diversity within epistemology that is not motivated by profit, but supplemented by the dissolution of essentialist identities and the creation of a new universality across the marginalised?

Access to information and the diversity of voices is something for which the marginalised continue to fight in today's age. This is a commendable fight that must be propagated by all means necessary. However, the intersectionality of marginalisation must be supplemented with the problem of equal access to technology and the right to produce (not only consume) information. The traumatic position of the marginalised must be acknowledged, and all kinds of myths pertaining to an equal start must be dispelled. In turn, marginalisation should not result in a multiplicity of atomised identities, each of which compete to shout among the noise. While it takes the form of a multiplicity, one must acknowledge the universality of oppression and alienation itself. Simply put, a new structure of epistemology must be one that celebrates diversity without essentialising a sanctity of diverse knowledge.

2. The Political Question: How can we achieve a fairer distribution of the material substrates of power, i.e. wealth, technology, and ownership of data, to build new spaces of technological play?

Of course, such a system will only come to its full potential once we take into account the distribution of the material substrates of power. Data gathering as such, while fundamentally dis/individualising, does not have to lead to an inherently violent society. It is our powerlessness in regards to how our data is collected and how it will be used that is the problem. It is how a loss of privacy is presented as an unnegotiable price to pay for our comfort that is the problem. We believe that new spaces of technological play must be made outside of selfish monolithic enclosures of singular tech giants that ultimately subsume everything under the profit motive. In this ideal world we strive for, netizens become bricoleurs as pieces of technology are released from their corporate shells, roaming freely like Lego bricks ready to be assembled for various problem-solving and entertainment purposes.

3. The Economic Question: How can we create an economy that does not valorise social antagonism for the wealth of the ruling class but can generate real wealth for the general populace?

By its very nature, digital technology that connects people to one another will always bring the Other into over-proximity. The neighbour's *jouissance* will always make itself visible, serving as a source of trauma, hatred, and anxiety. Antagonism is constitutive of society as such, and will persist no matter how much technology is utilised. However, to exploit this antagonism as a source of profit is another thing. Sharpening the clashes within and between communities into razor-sharp blades that cut at the very psyche of its constituents, creating massive waves of anxiety and depression in the name of 'engagement' that serve nothing but to put more money in the hands of a few global billionaires, is an egregious violence. While we do not know what a future political economy might look like, we must demand that it is not one driven by an engine of hatred towards the Other's *jouissance*.

We deliberately phrase each of the three points above not as demands but as questions for the reader's imagination. What we are attempting is neither solution nor programme, but simply interrogations that we hope can begin to open new possibilities. Like the Borromean knot, the three are inextricably linked together; when one slips away, so will the other two. Epistemic justice cannot be achieved if power is still concentrated in the hands of the few and antagonisms are deliberately sharpened. A distribution of power will fail if epistemological narratives are still dominated by the ruling class that relish in our infighting. Finally, an alternative economy will not function if knowledge is still written by the most powerful, and the most powerful still hold on to the sources of their power. Each of the three needs to be imagined together and fought for in an effort as concerted as a society possibly can.

The three *loci* are neither name nor master signifier. What we are proposing is instead a new topology—a collective effort to reorganise the epistemic, the political, and the economic. Within each of the three one can find a Real-Symbolic-Imaginary ternary, with the Symbolic slipping away as no master signifier can maintain their consistency in the dizzying infinite loop of capitalism. Instead of a new master signifier, then, we are proposing to imagine a new *sinthome* that connects the RSI chain in the epistemic-political-economic triad. All revolutions must start by imagining a new constellation of enjoyment in knowledge, politics, and value creation that does not depend on the suffering of others, for it is only then that we can begin to invent a new universe.

This new universe, if and when we are able to invent it, will not be an ideal one. The sexual non-relationship, unless we somehow manage to evolve into a new species that transcends language or otherwise lose our subjectivity in a tragic accident, will most likely persist. Likewise, the non-relationship between our physical and digital lives will persist. We are a hole in ontology. Unfortunately, racism, misogyny, transphobia, ableism, and all sorts of bigotry will emerge in the panic of staring into such an abyss. Just like an outside observer finds themself unable to objectively discern the truth of an amorous relationship, the universe may look the same at first. We will be weary, we will be in panic, we will lose hope. As Mari Matsuda (2005, 190) says, 'We won't know we are winning this battle when we are in it.'

Nonetheless, if we have succeeded in our radical decision, it will be a new universe. Once it has been established, states of panic may decidedly shape the creation of the new universe and particular moments within it. But the new universe will be infused with an ambience and affectivity of the erotic. Once a radically new space has been created and the political and economic structures have been altered, the erotic will emerge and calm the panic without losing its fervour. We will welcome a new universe with open arms and profound alacrity, as we will finally be free in our playful interdependence with empathy. We will have invented a future, reclaiming true possibilities in place of finitude and exhaustion. We will have crossed the Event Horizon.

Author Biographies

Bonni Rambatan is an independent scholar and researcher based in Jakarta, Indonesia, as well as a writer and artist for various comics, novels, films, installations, and other media. They co-founded and currently run a comic book company, NaoBun, focusing on making progressive thoughts available to young readers. They started and edited the anthology *Cyborg Subjects: Discourses on Digital Culture* with Jacob Johanssen (CreateSpace, 2013).

Their research interests include Lacanian psychoanalysis, media studies, literary and art criticism, Japanese studies, philosophy, and critical theory. For research and artistic projects, their affiliations include The Japan Foundation, the Vienna-based art-technology-philosophy group monochrom, as well as various art and literary institutions in Indonesia.

Jacob Johanssen is Senior Lecturer in Communications at St Mary's University (London, UK). He is the author of *Psychoanalysis and Digital Culture: Audiences, Social Media, and Big Data* (Routledge, 2019); *Fantasy, Online Misogyny and the Manosphere: Male Bodies of Dis/Inhibition* (Routledge, 2021), and *Cyborg Subjects: Discourses on Digital Culture*, edited with Bonni Rambatan (CreateSpace, 2013).

His research interests include psychoanalysis and digital media, sexuality, and digital media, affect theories, psychosocial studies, and critical theory. He is Co-Editor of the Counterspace section of the journal *Psychoanalysis, Culture & Society*. He sits on the executive committee of the Association for Psychosocial Studies (APS). He is a Founder Scholar of the British Psychoanalytic Council (BPC).

Endnotes

1 We mostly use the Lacanian understanding of the Subject (about which we write with a capital S) throughout the book.

2 This book does not provide a detailed introduction to Lacanian thinking and we have kept these introductory notes brief in order to focus on the book's themes. Chapter 1 will delve further into Lacan's ideas but will not explain its origins in Freud's work for the same reason. For further exploration and other supplemental materials, please visit the book's website as stated on the cover pages.

3 Throughout this book, we use the term 'Alt-Right' in broad strokes to connote the wider spread of toxic ideas and communities online, such as the so-called Alt-Lite, the Intellectual Dark Web, the Dark Enlightenment, Neo-Reactionism (NRx), and Far Right accelerationism. It is beyond the scope of this book to discuss their ideas and how they overlap with and diverge from the Alt-Right in detail (see e.g. Sandifer 2017; Aikin 2018; Jones 2019 for discussions).

4 For more discussions on this concept, please refer to various works by Feldner and Vighi, e.g. (2018). More of the works will also be discussed in the following pages.

5 We should note that, with these examples, psychosis should not be taken literally in any clinical sense of the term—the psychotic of the clinic, for example, survives by creating signifiers that are meaningful to the Subject alone (Lacan 1989). We are here speaking of a structural resemblance. Additionally, while it might be tempting to read ideas of how we are living in a Matrix-style simulated universe as a form of delusion, it must be noted that these actually come closer to neurosis in the sense that the imagined

all-powerful Other has been completely stripped of their dimension of enjoyment. The higher beings (aliens, future civilisations, etc.) that simulate our universe hardly do so for their selfish gains and cruel laughter.

6 In his extensive discussion of the dream, Leonard Shengold makes a similar argument to ours. He links the dream to Freud's own history, even though Freud writes that the dream was told to him by a female patient who herself had heard about it in a lecture. The precise origins of the dream remain unknown. Nonetheless, Shengold highlights that Freud lost his brother when he was very young and his father when he was 41 years old. Shengold also links the dream to Freud's relationship with his father and his desire for recognition. Freud's father thought that the young Sigmund Freud would 'come to nothing' (Shengold 1991, 52).

7 Of course, this does not mean that there are no pessimist views and heated arguments within the queer community itself. What it means is that to engage in queer relationships is still contested and debated among e.g. bisexuals and lesbians, trans and non-binary people, asexual and polyamorous communities, queer-straight couples, and so on.

8 Of course, many women are actually queer and engage in straight relationships out of 'compulsory heterosexuality', as poet and essayist Adrienne Rich (1980) has written about. These women will undoubtedly have much more fulfilling experiences once they engage in queer relationships. We will also acknowledge that, for queer people finally coming out of the closet, their queer relationships are most likely indeed better than their previous relationships. In these discussions, however, we are talking strictly about the imagination that queer relationships are essentially better regardless of the nature of one's sexuality.

9   For a much more comprehensive discussion of the four works, refer to the blog blautoothdmand (2018). We have also followed the blog author's sequence in discussing the four works instead of the chronological order in the anthology since we feel it better portrays the escalating absurdity.

10   While addictive UX design can and does have a lot of negative impact on society, it is important not to demonise designers as a group with ill intent. In the Netflix documentary series *Abstract: The Art of Design* (Season 2 Episode 5), Aza Raskin, the designer of the infinite scroll, shows remorse regarding the feature. He realised too late that what he did was to 'remove the stopping cues…so it's literally wasted hundreds of millions of human hours'. Raskin regrets that he only thought of individual interactions instead of what he calls the level of 'technology-society interaction'. The episode also tackles the question of the designers of Instagram (and a mention of Twitter) grappling with the impact of their design that has caused an unhealthy obsession towards follower counts, as well as challenges designers face when there is pressure for more profit and hence more hook towards technology.

Bibliography

Aikin, S. F. (2019). Deep disagreement, the dark enlightenment, and the rhetoric of the red pill. *Journal of Applied Philosophy*, 36(3), 420-435.

Azuma, H. (2009). *Otaku. Japan's Database Animals*. Minneapolis, MN: University of Minnesota Press.

Badiou, A. (2006). *Being and Event*. New York: Continuum.

Badiou, A. (2008). The Communist Hypothesis. *New Left Review*, 49, 29-42.

Banet-Weiser, S. (2018). *Empowered: Popular Feminism and Popular Misogyny*. Durham, NC: Duke University Press.

Bidet, J. (2016). *Foucault with Marx*. London: Zed Books.

Blautoothdmand (2018). Reflections on Shintaro Kago's panel experiments. https://blautoothdmand.wordpress.com/2018/11/18/reflections-on-shintaro-kagos-panel-experiments/.

Bratich, J. and Banet-Weiser, S. (2019). From Pick-up Artists to Incels: Con(fidence) Games, Networked Misogyny, and the Failure of Neoliberalism. *International Journal of Communication*, 13, 5003–5027.

Bucher, T. (2012). The friendship assemblage: Investigating programmed sociality on Facebook. *Television & New Media*, 14(6), 479-493.

Buckels, E. E., Trapnell, P. D. and Paulhus, D. L. (2014). Trolls just want to have fun. *Personality and Individual Differences*, 67, 97-102.

Chabin, M. (2018). Horror and the Big Elsewhere: Traumatic Enjoyment in Event Horizon and True Detective. *Clues: A Journal of Detection*, 36(2), 82-90.

Christie's. Takashi Murakami (b. 1962). Hiropon. https://www.christies.com/lotfinder/Lot/takashi-murakami-b-1962-hiropon-3914610-details.aspx.

Chun, W. H. K. (2016). *Updating to Remain the Same: Habitual New Media*. Minneapolis: University of Minnesota Press.

Citarella, J. (2019). Irony Politics & Gen Z. https://newmodels. io/proprietary/irony-politics-gen-z-2019-citarella

Clarke, A.C. (1973). *Profiles of the Future: An Inquiry into the Limits of the Possible*. New York: Harper & Row.

CREA. (1992). Magazine. November 1992.

Dean, J. (2010). *Blog Theory: Feedback and Capture in the Circuits of Drive*. Cambridge: Polity.

Douglas, S. (2011). How Much is Too Much? Murakami's Prices. *Observer*. https://observer.com/2011/07/how-much-is-too-much-murakamis-prices/.

Drohojowska-Philp, H. (2001). Superflat. *Artnet*. http://www. artnet.com/magazine/features/drohojowska-philp/drohojowska-philp1-18-01.asp.

Edelman, L. (2013). Sex Without Optimism. In Berlant, L. and Edelman, L. *Sex, or the Unbearable*. Durham, NC: Duke University Press.

Estavillo, E. C. (2012). *The PSN Plaintiff: A Biography*. Seattle, MA: Kindle Books.

Feldner, H. and Vighi, F. (2018). Finitude of Capitalism and the Perverse Charm of Denial. *Berlin Journal of Critical Theory* 2(2), 99-130.

Finn, E. (2017). *What Algorithms Want: Imagination in the Age of Computing*. Cambridge, MA: MIT Press.

Firdaus, F. (2020). Global protests throw spotlight on alleged police abuses in West Papua. *The Guardian*. https://www. theguardian.com/global-development/2020/jun/11/global-protests-throw-spotlight-on-alleged-police-abuses-in-west-papua

Fisher, M. (2006). Reflexive Impotence. *K-Punk*. http://k-punk. abstractdynamics.org/archives/007656.html.

Fisher, M. (2009). *Capitalist Realism. Is There no Alternative?* Winchester: Zero Books.

Fisher, M. (2013). Exiting the Vampire Castle's. *openDemocracy*. https://www.opendemocracy.net/en/opendemocracyuk/exiting-vampire-castle/.

Fisher, M. (2014). *Ghosts of My Life. Writings on Depression, Hauntology and Lost Futures*. Winchester: Zer0 Books.

Foucault, M. (1977). *Discipline and Punish: The Birth of the Prison*. New York: Vintage Books.

Foucault, M. (1978). *The History of Sexuality. Volume 1: An Introduction*. New York: Pantheon Books.

Freud, S. (1981). The Interpretation of Dreams. *The Standard Edition of the Complete Psychological Works of Sigmund Freud. Volume V. The interpretations of Dreams (Second Part) and On Dreams*. London: The Hogarth Press and the Institute of Psycho-Analysis.

Frosh, S. (2010). *Psychoanalysis Outside the Clinic: Interventions in Psychosocial Studies*. Basingstoke: Palgrave Macmillan.

Gates, B. (2015). The next outbreak? We're not ready. *TED talk*. https://www.ted.com/talks/bill_gates_the_next_outbreak_we_re_not_ready?language=en.

Glück, L. (2005). Foreword. In Siken, R. (2005). *Crush*. New Haven, CT: Yale University Press, pp. vii-xi.

Gstalter, M. (2019). Milo Yiannopoulos named marshal for 'Straight Pride' parade. The Hill. https://thehill.com/blogs/blog-briefing-room/news/447553-milo-yiannopoulos-named-marshal-for-straight-pride-parade.

Gutierrez, C. (2016). The Other Self in Free Fall: Anxiety and Automated Tracking Applications. *CM: Communication and Media*, 11, 38, pp. 111–134.

Hale, T. (2017). This Viral Video Of A Racist Soap Dispenser Reveals A Much, Much Bigger Problem. *IFL Science*. https://www.iflscience.com/technology/this-racist-soap-dispenser-reveals-why-diversity-in-tech-is-muchneeded/.

Han, B.-C. (2015). *The Burnout Society*. Paolo Alto, CA: Stanford University Press.

Han, B.-C. (2017). *Psychopolitics. Neoliberalism and New Technologies of Power*. London: Verso.

Haraway, D. (1991). A Cyborg Manifesto: Science, Technology, and Socialist-Feminism in the Late Twentieth Century. In: *Simians, Cyborgs and Women: The Reinvention of Nature*. London: Routledge, pp.149-181.

Hawley, G. (2017). *Making Sense of the Alt-Right*. New York: Columbia University Press.

Hayles, N. K. (1999). *How We Became Posthuman: Virtual Bodies in Cybernetics, Literature, and Informatics*. Chicago, IL: University of Chicago Press.

Hayles, N. K. (2008). *Electronic Literature: New Horizons for the Literary*. Notre Dame, IN: University of Notre Dame Press.

Healey, K. and Potter, R. (2018). Coding the Privileged Self: Facebook and the Ethics of Psychoanalysis 'Outside the Clinic'. *Television & New Media*, 19(7), 660-676.

Hill, K. (2012). How Target Figured Out A Teen Girl Was Pregnant Before Her Father Did. Forbes. https://www.forbes.com/sites/kashmirhill/2012/02/16/how-target-figured-out-a-teen-girl-was-pregnant-before-her-father-did/.

Homer, S. (2005). *Jacques Lacan*. London: Routledge.

Hook, D. and Vanheule, S. (2016). Revisiting the Master-Signifier, or, Mandela and Repression. *Frontiers in Psychology*, https://www.frontiersin.org/articles/10.3389/fpsyg.2015.02028/full.

Johanssen, J. (2019). *Psychoanalysis and Digital Culture: Audiences, Social Media, and Big Data*. London: Routledge.

Johanssen, J. (2021). *Fantasy, Online Misogyny and the Manosphere: Male Bodies of Dis/Inhibition*. London: Routledge.

Jones, A. (2019). From NeoReactionary Theory to the Alt-Right. In: Battista, C. M. and Sande, M. R. (Eds.): *Critical Theory and the Humanities in the Age of the Alt-Right*. Basingstoke: Palgrave Macmillan, 101-120.

Kago, S. (2004). *Kasutoru Shiki*. Tokyo: Ohta Shuppan.

Kale, S. (2018). Erectile dysfunction or performance anxiety? The

truth behind a modern malaise. *The Guardian*. https://www.
theguardian.com/lifeandstyle/2018/oct/18/erectile-dysfunc-
tion-performance-anxiety-truth-modern-malaise.

Kasperkevic, J. (2015). Google says sorry for racist auto-tag in
photo app. *The Guardian*. https://www.theguardian.com/
technology/2015/jul/01/google-sorry-racist-auto-tag-photo-
app.

Keating, S. (2019). The Year in Heteropessimism. *BuzzFeed*.
https://www.buzzfeednews.com/article/shannonkeating/
straight-romance-heteropessimism-marriage-story.

Kinsella, S. (1995). Cuties in Japan. In: Moeran, B. and Skov,
L. (Eds.). *Women, Media and Consumption in Japan*. London:
Routledge, pp. 220-254.

Krüger, S. and Johanssen, J. (2016). Thinking (with) the unconscious in media and communication studies: Introduction
to the special issue. CM: *Communication and Media Journal*,
11(38), 5-40.

Lacan, J. (1978). *Lacan in Italia. 1953-1978. En Italie Lacan*. Milan:
La Salmandra.

Lacan, J. (1989). Kant with Sade. *October* 51 (Winter, 1989), 55-
75.

Lacan, J. (1993). *The Seminar of Jacques Lacan. Book III. The Psycho-
ses. 1955-56*. New York: W. W. Norton & Company.

Lacan, J. (1998). *The Seminar of Jacques Lacan. Book XIII. The Object of Psychoanalysis. 1965-66*. New York: W. W. Norton &
Company.

Lacan, J. (1999). *The Seminar of Jacques Lacan. Book XX. Encore:
On Feminine Sexuality, the Limits of Love and Knowledge. 1972-
73*. New York: W.W. Norton & Company.

Lacan, J. (2002). Ècrits. New York: W. W. Norton & Company.

Lacan, J. (2007). *The Seminar of Jacques Lacan. Seminar XVII. The
Other Side of Psychoanalysis. 1969-70*. New York: W. W. Norton & Company.

Lizza, R. (2017). How Alt-Right 'Fellow-Traveller' Milo Yiannopoulos Cracked Up the Right. *The New Yorker.* https://www.newyorker.com/news/ryan-lizza/how-alt-right-fellow-traveller-milo-yiannopoulos-cracked-up-the-right

Lorde, A. (1984). The Uses of the Erotic. The Erotic as Power. In Lovaas, K. and Jenkins, M. M. (eds.). *Everyday Life: A Reader.* London: Sage, pp. 87-91.

Lovink, G. (2011). *Networks without a Cause. A Critique of Social Media.* Cambridge: Polity Press.

Lovink, G. (2019). *Sad by Design. On Platform Nihilism.*

MacDougald , P. (2019). Cat People. Tablet Mag. https://www.tabletmag.com/sections/arts-letters/articles/cat-people-roupenian.

Mannoni, O. (1969). Je sais bien, mais quand même. *Clefs pour l'Imaginaire ou l'Autre Scène.* Paris: Seuil, pp. 9-33.

Manovich, L. (2001). *The Language of New Media.* New Haven, MA: MIT press.

Marx, K. (1992). *Capital: A Critique of Political Economy. Vol. 1.* New York: Penguin.

Matsuda, M. (2005). Love, Change. *Yale Journal of Law & Feminism, 17,* 185-203.

May, S. (2019). *The Power of Cute.* Princeton, NJ: Princeton University Press.

McCloud, S. (1993). *Understanding Comics: The Invisible Art.* Northampton, MA: Tundra Publishing.

Murakami, T. (2005). Earth in my Window. In: Murakami, T. (Ed.). *Little Boy: The Arts of Japan's Exploding Subculture.* New Haven, CT: Yale University Press, pp. 100-101.

Nagle, A. (2017). *Kill All Normies. Online Culture Wars from 4chan and Tumblr to Trump and the Alt-Right.* Winchester: Zer0 Books.

Nakamura, L. (2002). *Cybertypes.* New York: Routledge

Negri, A. (2017). *Marx and Foucault. Essays Volume I.* Cambridge: Polity Press.

Ngai, S. (2005). The Cuteness of the Avant-Garde. *Critical In-*

quiry 31(4), 811-847.

No Author. (2017). The world's most valuable resource is no longer oil, but data. *The Economist*. https://www.economist.com/leaders/2017/05/06/the-worlds-most-valuable-resource-is-no-longer-oil-but-data.

Ortega, R. R. (2020). Sex addict sues Amazon-owned video platform Twitch for $25million because it has 'too many scantily clad gamers' that left him excited and he 'injured himself'. https://www.dailymail.co.uk/news/article-8461643/Sex-addict-sues-video-platform-Twitch-25million-scantily-clad-gamers.html.

O'Brien, L. (2020). The Far-Right Helped Create The World's Most Powerful Facial Recognition Technology. *The Huffington Post*. https://www.huffingtonpost.ca/entry/clearview-ai-facial-recognition-alt-right.

O'Neill, R. (2018). *Seduction: Men, Masculinity and Mediated Intimacy*. London: John Wiley & Sons.

Penny, L. (2018). Who does she think she is? *Longreads*. https://longreads.com/2018/03/28/who-does-she-think-she-is/.

Piatetsky, G. (2014). Did Target Really Predict a Teen's Pregnancy? The Inside Story. KDnuggets. https://www.kdnuggets.com/2014/05/target-predict-teen-pregnancy-inside-story.html.

Przybylo, E. (2019). *Asexual Erotics: Intimate Readings of Compulsory Sexuality*. Columbia, OH: The Ohio State University Press.

Rich, A. (1980). Compulsory heterosexuality and lesbian existence. *Signs: Journal of Women in Culture and Society*, 5(4), 631-660.

Rogers, R. (2019). 'My wife asked me…'. Twitter. https://twitter.com/richrogers_/status/1134973002196574209.

Romano, A. (2020). How K-pop fans are weaponizing the internet for Black Lives Matter. Vox. https://www.vox.com/2020/6/8/21279262/k-pop-fans-black-lives-matter-fancams-youtubers-protest-support.

Roupenian, K. (2017). Cat Person. *The New Yorker.* https://www. newyorker.com/magazine/2017/12/11/cat-person.

Sales, N. J. (2015). Tinder and the Dawn of the 'Dating Apocalypse'. *Vanity Fair.* https://www.vanityfair.com/ culture/2015/08/tinder-hook-up-culture-end-of-dating.

Sandifer, E. (2017). *Neoreaction. A Basilisk. Essays on and Around the Alt-Right.* Danbury, CT: Eruditorum Press.

Santner, E. L. (1996). *My Own Private Germany. Daniel Paul Schreber's Secret History of Modernity.* Princeton, NJ: Princeton University Press.

Schwarz, J. and Biddle, S. (2019). For Some Reason, We Can't Find a Single Leftist Mark Zuckerberg Invited to His Dinners With Pundits From 'Across the Spectrum'. *The Intercept.* https://theintercept.com/2019/10/25/mark-zuckerberg-facebook-dinners/.

Seresin, I. (2019). On Heteropessimism. *The New Inquiry.* https:// thenewinquiry.com/on-heteropessimism/.

Seymour, R. (2019). *The Twittering Machine.* The Indigo Press.

Shengold, L. (1991). *Father, Don't You See I'm Burning: Reflections on Sex, Narcissism, Symbolism, and Murder: From Everything to Nothing.* New Haven, CT: Yale University Press.

Siken, R. (2005). *Crush.* New Haven, CT: Yale University Press.

Spiegel, E. (2015). What is Snapchat? YouTube. https://www. youtube.com/watch?v=ykGXIQAHLnA&feature=youtu.be.

Tomšič, S. (2018). *The Capitalist Unconscious.* London: Verso.

Turkle, S. (2011). *Alone Together: Why We Expect More from Technology and Less from Each Other.* New York: Basic Books.

Varagur, K. (2020). Black Lives Matter in Indonesia, Too. *Foreign Policy.* https://foreignpolicy.com/2020/06/16/black-lives-matter-papua-indonesia/

Warren, K. (2020). Jeff Bezos has gotten $70 billion richer in the past 12 months. Here are 11 mind-blowing facts that show just how wealthy the Amazon CEO really is. *Business Insid-*

er. https://www.businessinsider.com/how-rich-is-jeff-bezos-mind-blowing-facts-net-worth-2019-4.

What's your opinion on Projekt Melody? https://incels.co/threads/whats-your-opinion-on-projekt-melody.208575/.

Yiannopoulos, M. (2011). Why I'll probably never be a parent. https://web.archive.org/web/20110714053205/http://yiannopoulos.net/2011/07/11/why-ill-probably-never-be-a-parent/.

Žižek, S. (1989). *The Sublime Object of Ideology*. London: Verso.

Žižek, S. (2017). Ideology Is the Original Augmented Reality. Nautilus. http://nautil.us/issue/54/the-unspoken/ideology-is-the-original-augmented-reality.

Žižek, S. (2019). They Are Both Worse. *The Philosophical Salon*. https://thephilosophicalsalon.com/they-are-both-worse/.

Zupančič, A. (2017). *What is Sex?* New Haven, MA: MIT Press.

Films

Abstract: The Art of Design. 2017. Various directors.

Behind the Curve. 2018. Directed by Daniel J. Clark.

Cam. 2018. Directed by Daniel Goldhaber.

Event Horizon. 1997. Directed by Paul W. S. Anderson.

Her. 2013. Directed by Spike Jonze.

The Great Hack. 2019. Directed by Jehane Noujaim and Karim Amer.

The Social Dilemma. 2020. Directed by Jeff Orlowski.

You. 2018. Various directors.

CULTURE, SOCIETY & POLITICS

The modern world is at an impasse. Disasters scroll across our smartphone screens and we're invited to like, follow or upvote, but critical thinking is harder and harder to find. Rather than connecting us in common struggle and debate, the internet has sped up and deepened a long-standing process of alienation and atomization. Zer0 Books wants to work against this trend. With critical theory as our jumping off point, we aim to publish books that make our readers uncomfortable. We want to move beyond received opinions.

Zer0 Books is on the left and wants to reinvent the left. We are sick of the injustice, the suffering and the stupidity that defines both our political and cultural world, and we aim to find a new foundation for a new struggle.

If this book has helped you to clarify an idea, solve a problem or extend your knowledge, you may want to check out our online content as well. Look for Zer0 Books: Advancing Conversations in the iTunes directory and for our Zer0 Books YouTube channel.

Popular videos include:
Žižek and the Double Blackmain
The Intellectual Dark Web is a Bad Sign
Can there be an Anti-SJW Left?
Answering Jordan Peterson on Marxism

Follow us on Facebook
at https://www.facebook.com/ZeroBooks and Twitter at https://twitter.com/Zer0Books

Bestsellers from Zer0 Books include:

Give Them An Argument
Logic for the Left
Ben Burgis
Many serious leftists have learned to distrust talk of logic. This is
a serious mistake.
Paperback: 978-1-78904-210-8 ebook: 978-1-78904-211-5

Poor but Sexy
Culture Clashes in Europe East and West
Agata Pyzik
How the East stayed East and the West stayed West.
Paperback: 978-1-78099-394-2 ebook: 978-1-78099-395-9

An Anthropology of Nothing in Particular
Martin Demant Frederiksen
A journey into the social lives of meaninglessness.
Paperback: 978-1-78535-699-5 ebook: 978-1-78535-700-8

In the Dust of This Planet
Horror of Philosophy vol. 1
Eugene Thacker
In the first of a series of three books on the Horror of Philosophy,
In the Dust of This Planet offers the genre of horror as a way of
thinking about the unthinkable.
Paperback: 978-1-84694-676-9 ebook: 978-1-78099-010-1

The End of Oulipo?
An Attempt to Exhaust a Movement
Lauren Elkin, Veronica Esposito
Paperback: 978-1-78099-655-4 ebook: 978-1-78099-656-1

Capitalist Realism
Is There No Alternative?
Mark Fisher
An analysis of the ways in which capitalism has presented itself
as the only realistic political-economic system.
Paperback: 978-1-84694-317-1 ebook: 978-1-78099-734-6

Rebel Rebel
Chris O'Leary
David Bowie: every single song. Everything you want to know,
everything you didn't know.
Paperback: 978-1-78099-244-0 ebook: 978-1-78099-713-1

Kill All Normies
Angela Nagle
Online culture wars from 4chan and Tumblr to Trump.
Paperback: 978-1- 78535-543-1 ebook: 978-1-78535-544-8

Cartographies of the Absolute
Alberto Toscano, Jeff Kinkle
An aesthetics of the economy for the twenty-first century.
Paperback: 978-1-78099-275-4 ebook: 978-1-78279-973-3

Malign Velocities
Accelerationism and Capitalism
Benjamin Noys
Long listed for the Bread and Roses Prize 2015, *Malign Velocities*
argues against the need for speed, tracking acceleration
as the symptom of the ongoing crises of capitalism.
Paperback: 978-1-78279-300-7 ebook: 978-1-78279-299-4

Meat Market
Female Flesh under Capitalism
Laurie Penny
A feminist dissection of women's bodies as the fleshy fulcrum of capitalist cannibalism, whereby women are both consumers and consumed.
Paperback: 978-1-84694-521-2 ebook: 978-1-84694-782-7

Babbling Corpse
Vaporwave and the Commodification of Ghosts
Grafton Tanner
Paperback: 978-1-78279-759-3 ebook: 978-1-78279-760-9

New Work New Culture
Work we want and a culture that strengthens us
Frithjoff Bergmann
A serious alternative for mankind and the planet.
Paperback: 978-1-78904-064-7 ebook: 978-1-78904-065-4

Romeo and Juliet in Palestine
Teaching Under Occupation
Tom Sperlinger
Life in the West Bank, the nature of pedagogy and the role of a university under occupation.
Paperback: 978-1-78279-637-4 ebook: 978-1-78279-636-7

Ghosts of My Life
Writings on Depression, Hauntology and Lost Futures
Mark Fisher
Paperback: 978-1-78099-226-6 ebook: 978-1-78279-624-4

Sweetening the Pill

or How We Got Hooked on Hormonal Birth Control
Holly Grigg-Spall
Has contraception liberated or oppressed women?
Sweetening the Pill breaks the silence on the dark side of hormonal
contraception.
Paperback: 978-1-78099-607-3 ebook: 978-1-78099-608-0

Why Are We The Good Guys?

Reclaiming Your Mind from the Delusions of Propaganda
David Cromwell
A provocative challenge to the standard ideology that Western
power is a benevolent force in the world.
Paperback: 978-1-78099-365-2 ebook: 978-1-78099-366-9

The Writing on the Wall

On the Decomposition of Capitalism and its Critics
Anselm Jappe, Alastair Hemmens
A new approach to the meaning of social emancipation.
Paperback: 978-1-78535-581-3 ebook: 978-1-78535-582-0

Most titles are published in paperback and as an ebook.
Paperbacks are available in traditional bookshops. Both print and
ebook formats are available online.
Follow us on Facebook
at https://www.facebook.com/ZeroBooks
and Twitter at https://twitter.com/Zer0Books